SPIT WITH A PURPOSE
PRESENTS

"OUTCREYE"
VOL. II

SPIT WITH A PURPOSE
PRESENTS

"OUTCREYE"
VOL. II

By Robert Rush

Published by
MIDNIGHT EXPRESS BOOKS

SPIT WITH A PURPOSE
PRESENTS

"OUTCREYE"
VOL. II

(THE LINE-UP)

REESE

OMAR

LIL BOO

ACE

I-SUN

RAMON

SHORT

ZELLE

U-WISE

LOS

AHMOSE

ANT

KUTA

OUT CREYE Vol. II
Copyright © 2012 by Robert K. Rush

ISBN-10: 0984744479
ISBN-13: 978-0-9847444-7-3

Published by
MIDNIGHT EXPRESS BOOKS
POBox 69
Berryville AR 72616
(870) 210-3772
MEBooks1@yahoo.com

SPIT WITH A PURPOSE

PRESENTS

"OUTCREYE"
VOL. II

By Robert Rush

Spit With a Purpose

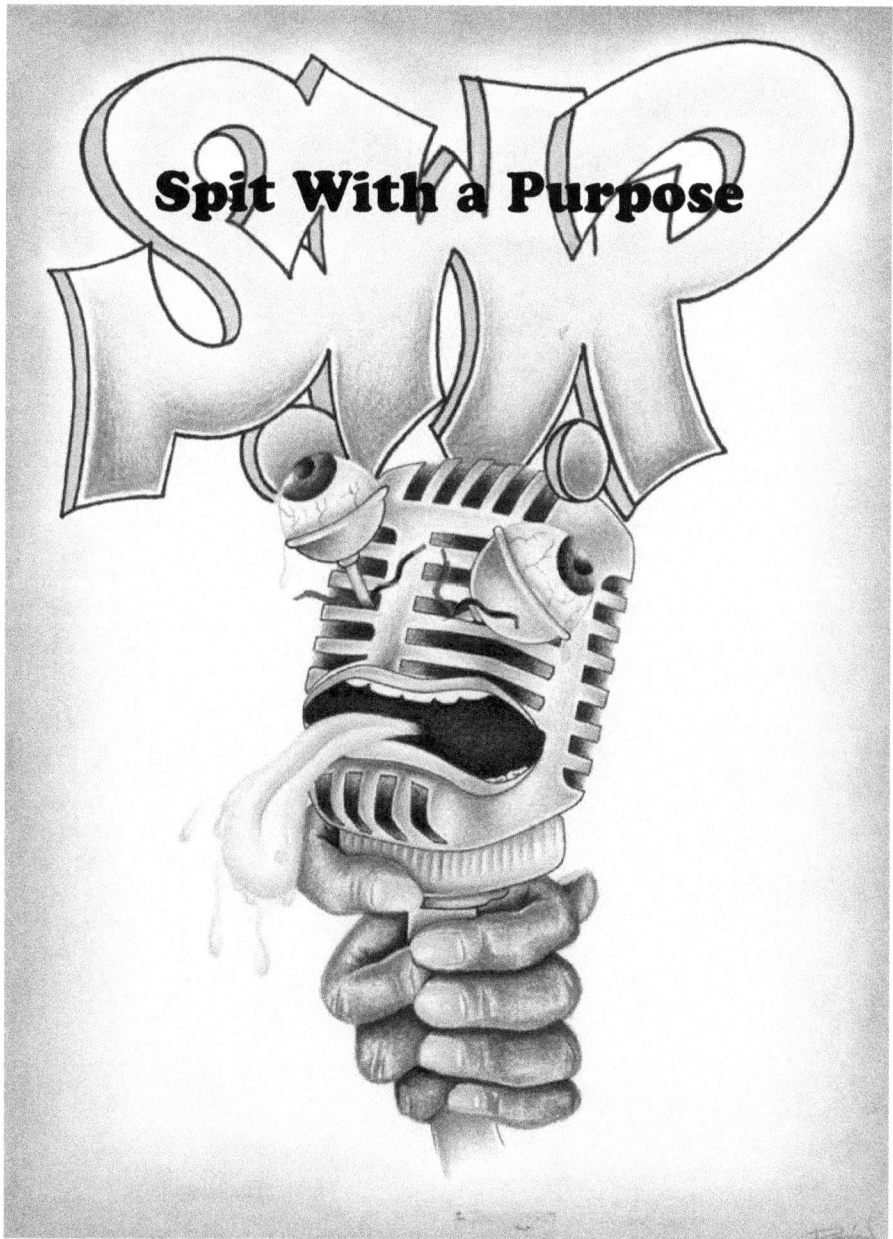

Art by Ramon

Acknowledgements

God first! Thank you for the mind and gifts that abides in me. I'm so grateful for the spirit you've created within my fractured being.

Thank you Mom for stirring those gifts. Thank you Dad for your wisdom and wits.

A huge shout out to my big sis, Tanna Moore for always supporting me. Much love to my lil sis Dawn rush and my brother, Edward Rush.

Shout out to the Queens, Ashley Shellman and Micah Rush. I want to give a special thanks to every artist that participated in this book. This one is for ya'll.

Zelle, Ramon, Reese, K.T., Lil Boo, Rio, I-Sun U-wise, Ace, Memfis, Los, Omar, Ahmose, Short, Hassan, Ant, and Conscientious. I got mad respect for all of you dudes for trusting me with your thoughts.

Peace to the young men and woman that are in prison. Like Short said:

> "Our minds are transitioned to pop locks," meaning, we can open the doors of opportunity if we were to utilize our minds. "Freedom is knowledge."

A special thanks to Midnight Express Books for their hard work on this endeavor.

It's a must that I honor my Star, Joyce Wison---"I Love You."

Also I want to give honor to Constance Stanley, you're loved as well.

I can't end this without sending love to my foundation, Romana Rice for always holding me down, you know what it is.

What up to the Wilborns and the Morans, too many to name.

What up to all my homies in Menard, Statesville, and the River.

What up to the "Boogie" E. St. Louis. And to all the homies that's been missing in action for years, peace!

Luv to:

Shelley M.	Stan	Wayne	John John
Tracy C.	Rio	Muntin	Demarco
Beth O.	K.B.	Bo	Frenchie
Tish S.	Ce-Ce	Ray	Tone
Tasha W.	Percy	Tez	3 am.
Decenda W.	Nike	Sidney	Mack
Victoria S.	Bishop	Sarge	Champ & Teresa
Jennifer C.	Enrique	J.J.	Devin
Tammi L.	Ardi	Head	G-man
Kaila B.	Blue	D.B.	Red
Tiffany M.	Big Mane	Charlie	Shine
Ke-Ke	J-mac	Toby	Candi

R.I.P. Blink, June Bug, Kenneth and Black Season.

Foreword

"They fought like warrior poets." In the film Braveheart, the narrator describes the passion in which the Scottish fought the English under the rule of the unjustly cruel, tyrannical and often paranoid King Edward Long Shank. The Scottish fought against what was thought to be an undefeatable foe. They fought to be respected, to be regarded, they fought to be free.

Being something of a poet myself, the term "warrior poets" leapt out at me. More than just a crafty play off words the term held a much deeper meaning. It struck a personal note. Needling at my spirit I carried these haunting words with me down the long and twisting dirt road of life until at last I found the proper suitors. Just the right men to do the term justice. The poets of the book "Out Creye Vol II (The line-up)..." nothing felt more natural.

Anyone who has had the good fortune of sitting in the company of these gents will agree----they are without doubt, warriors! They are gladiators. Every writing one of them a captive.... fighting with office depot note pads for shields and ink-pens for swords. Their thoughts like fire lit bow and arrows and their tongues spiked-balls attached to 6 foot long iron chains. They too write for freedom.

I crossed paths with these gods of war during my stay at an Illinois Correctional Facility. I sat in complete and utter awe as I listened with both heart and soul to their poetic cries. I thought to myself this is more than just rhythmical composition. This is more than just poetry. This is revolt. I knew almost immediately that these captives were writing to be free. They were writing for their spirits to be heard. Each of them. They write with quiet anger. Their hurt is unnerving. Kuta, Reese, U-Wise, Zelle, and others, that brother in the darkest corner of the furthest cell, he too writes to be free.

These writers are of a different breed. I say to anyone who reads this book, who shares in the passion, the pain, the anger, the sorrow and triumph, who experiences the beautiful brilliance of these poems...read with your hearts rather than your minds. This is food for your soul. Eat, drink and quench that thirst that only true warriors know. Share these poems with someone you know. Live in the bountilessness of poetry. Freedom!

By: Willie Jackson

SPIT WITH A PURPOSE....

I pen my plasma through plastic & amass it on dead trees.
Transform it into acid & secrete classic master pieces.
My embodiment emphatically roam through passages
reserved to preserve literary sculptures,
but I reverse normalcy & nosedive into an airfield of airmen
who fly above the radar.
I write from the Russian Space station
and since my star outshines the supernova
I must be poetically Hova.
It was from state's property that I properly assembled a line up
that I'll line up
against any line up
that line up against us!
It was from the back of my mind that I adhered to the sign
that directed me back, to the back of my mind,
and If you don't mind,
I'll humbly turn my back to any line
aligned to undermine the never ending reign that destiny designed.
This astonishing association of lyrical domination is divine.
The Gods that the Universe answers to has anointed us Kings of Kings
and when there's a team of Kings esteemed intellectually with lyrical
prowess,
we render remedial poets powerless.
Our takeover began yesterday
and if yester had a year then rest restlessly because yesteryear is here!
I'm definitely what you should fear,
but my physical brut-ness is mediocre compared to my mental astuteness.
I kicked field goals to hustle the flow, to hustle the pen-stroke & to
hustle the antidote
to presumptuous cynics intent on witnessing the fall of Goliath
(such liars!)
and if Sampson slapped me I'll extract a lock & weave a tail,
assuring his ass that I'm too big to fail.
I'm too big like a cemetery filled with murdered kids
and the reeking reminisce of missing men spawned from the remnant of
missing men.

Fool's men mis-educating the development of mini-men
continuously & viciously snatching the life out of mini-men.
See, I'm linked to many men that rep the community.
We orchestrate spirituals on scrolls encircled in time
and since time is infinite, our portals are immortal,
so even in death we live similar to the spirit of lost innocence.
My voice resurrect the memories of every mini-me memorialized on a
rock
and since Spit With a Purpose has the purpose to uplift the block,
I'mma spit like my life depends on it
and in the event that my life ends on it.
My plasma will repaint the surface assuring all those who witnessed that I
lived & died... Spitting with a purpose!

SPIT WITH A PURPOSE...

The art we spit is not saliva but words
that come from the heart's pit
like hot lava emerge, and
these poetic topics disturb the logic preferred by those who envision
a perfect world in its worst condition.
I never seen a perfect politician,
a perfect Muslim,
nor a perfect Christian.
Lives are lost during rescue missions.
To lift my disposition,
I play good songs by cursed musicians.
Please understand it was my worst decision
to have my body locked in this position.
So, when redefining my mental definition,
don't give me any help. It's stupid to petition someone else.
My only competition is myself.
I'm two heavy weights in one
both fighting for the belt.
In the past,
I spit what I felt.
So much material lost---
I spit a bookshelf,
and I spit on everything
from poverty to wealth.
God bless my health for many years.
spit on fear...
In the White House,
my spit touched the President's ear.
I spit to bring us near,
close the spaces
In our communities (places) where
freebase is.
Briefcases of yayo...
Spit on the faces of racists----
taste this mayo.
You either wear the devil's horns
or the halo.

it's your choice.
I spit for those with no voice.
They hate it when I holler.
I'm dedicated---
Spit for them dollars, and if the crowd's educated,
spit like a scholar.
Iconic verses---
spitting earthless---Universe-ish,
or I can bring it back down to the surface
and spit at the serpent
because it's worthless, but this here is spitting with a purpose...

The warm up

Spit With a Purpose...

And I emerge with this conscious conversation for the
congregation
as my words string symphonies---
no sympathy, we're soldiers.
Catatonically comatose to your pessimistic notions,
which means your words are worthless.
We merge verbs into verses,
and victoriously deliver a spectacular speech,
such as "My Mother Don't Know Me" or "
I drowned In Katrina's Water"
in that "Epitome of Time" over looking God's wrath
from the "Roof Top" with a "Frozen Sun."
The chosen ones have come to the calling
and for our fallen we "OutCreye" again,
a second wind, but still on my first breath.
My first steps is toward salvation.
BET warned me to save myself,
so I purposely pen and pad my life's storms, and Pyrex jar poems that
come back dope.
I'm life's hope.
The Pope ain't the only one that knows Christ's secrets,
for whose reasons I write deeper.
He who seeks truth is still seeking
as I'm peeking pass the past life,
pass-ons pass messages that translate into atrocities.
Our planet in peril and the pavement is plagued with catastrophe.
There's got to be more than me that sees that somewhere lies a purpose
and that's why I spit...

Spit With a Purpose...

Rightfully so you're not alone,
the interpretation of the hieroglyphics were revealed through the lyrics of
a song.
My intuition gravitates me toward the writings on the walls of our homes,
with that
regurgitated verses spring from my lips with a God given purpose,
for the fetus curled up in its mother's womb
before you take your first breath or see the sun,
let these words create an eclipse between this world and that to come.
I spit it from the depths of my soul,
it fills your bones like marrow---
Sojourner the umbilical cord be the truth,
the purpose has always been for the youth.
Remove the Lexus coup,
the artist from the booth,
and I still stand tall when sitting to show the proof.
Ancestor's blood flowing through my veins,
like Obama I'm here to bring about change.
Keep a panhandler from change (nickels & dimes),
and through its feeding tube feed it tools to purchase a range.
I'm the intercession that's keeping us surfaced during the recession,
poverty has progression.
Gentrification is threatened in the wake of a depression.
C.P.R. will be performed poetically,
prophetically I learned the rebirth follows the hearse.
And no there's no curse,
check the rhythmic beats of your heart---
Now, tell me it's not a God.
I spit for those near and those afar (Haiti),
those without a car, those behind prison bars,
with dreams of being stars.
My purpose is to stop the hurting
within the lives of the little earthlings.
Purposely spitting with aim,
rearranging the functions of your brain.
Spit With a Purpose is the clique I claim.

Spit With a Purpose...

Reclaimed and unchained!
Intelligent minds shine to design peace and unbend the frame.
Spitting thee oppressor's harm,
I spit because my word is **Bond**!
The promise fulfilled....
My nation's to come.
Like unified rays of the sun
dawned the heart rate to vibrate,
in accord with voice boxes to regulate...
Photosynthesis!
As black genesis unfolds from souls oppressed,
synchronizing thoughts to rewrite revelations in futures flesh.
God blessed, yet eyes spit anger in stares of psychological
injustice,
tears spit fire like muskets,'
for slaves deemed capital---"Trust this..."
Bone shaking composure,
where bullwhips mold a...
Flock lost,--- "Chittlins-N-Hot Sauce!"
Hear my treble Peirce the navels of mother's with seeds
and bought,
sold before birth while the constitution constitutes my life as a write off.
Rehearsed in fertile soils;
pillage the mental & take our children for spoils,
in a war waged against our nature.
Trying to keep my cool as I inspire this paper,
but agony grows greater with vision of how they raped her.
"Damn those traders! ! !"
both black & white!
I spit pains from portions of a reality too real
to write!
From the drumming cry of every Native American Indian,
aligned with devastated generations of impoverished Africans.
"How dare you spit on the Motherland!"
With your greed filled eyes and material demand?!
So I spit to politic a change,

cause I'm tired of all this bullshit that seems
to rain from the media's reign,
painting my people insane.
Color me purple or color me God,
as I spit to hearts too hard to feel the devils dart.
The horn blown sharp to return us all,
to the rootless root & causeless cause.
Galaxies from afar applaud with awe,
as we spit spectrums of perfection as law.
Economically stable & no longer a fable,
I spit with magnetism drawing my people to the table!
But this is my word & my word is life,
bending time & shaping minds with my soul found light.
It was written by God and men alike.
Behold your "own" sight!
Written in birth as well as death.
which is why we spit these truths until the
universe captures our last breaths!

The warm up

Spit With a Purpose...

        I use words to spark the imagination
mixed the black love with brown pride
to create a deadly combination.
Once a lost soul until Spit With a Purpose
brought me to this poetic congregation.
I spit for the pride of my brown persuasion
with hopes to unite a misguided Puerto Rican nation
and if you didn't know-Humboldt Park is my location,
where killin' is as common as drug dealin'
and young brothaz dyin' over false identities,
leavin' no one to answer for the innocent blood that's spillin.
I represent for a beautiful race
that's divided by a code of silence and code of color.
How could you consciously decide to kill your brother
and break the heart of a woman who looks like your own mother?
Mi Jente, I know your struggle and your plight
and how some days we couldn't make it to school
without having to fight.
Even lived the struggle of growing up poor,
having to beg, borrow, and sometimes steal.
Witnessin' the harsh reality of watchin' my mom sell her body so that I
can have a meal.
And you think you live in fear?
I dare you to walk a mile in my shoes
without having to shed a tear.
The fear I have is not being afraid to die,
what scares me the most
is letting life pass me by.
PUT ME IN COACH...!!!
S.W.P. petitioned to send me on a mission,
word came from the top---dominate all competition.
S.W.P. should've meant spit with precision,
cause every stroke of my pen is something like a verbal circumcision...
man, listen...
Opportunity knocked in the form
of this spoken word.

Spit With a Purpose was my salvation
and it's with love that I spit every word.

Spit With a Purpose. . .

Boo, told me to go hard...
Wood is hard, but I'm one of the hardest, so...
I'm going steel----
my growing will
entices my symbolic saliva to spit at faces
like pumpkin off flavor of Love...
My behavior is bug,
When I'm spitting listen• my saliva is the Flavor of love, truth, peace,
freedom, & justice!
Meaning I am perpendicular
to a certain particular
group of people serving digits in the
prison system that's spitting the ...
Hardest shhh you ever heard.
With clever words
we together disturb
the masses whoever emerge
shall never deserve
to spit another poetic bar.
Forfeit or get ya door kicked...
that's how serious we take this poetical war shhh.
Please cease with the baby boobie
that King Kong squat and drop
cause we drop crazy dookie...
bodies imprisoned,
but minds transitioned
to pop the locks.
We own the keys & they are golden,
similar to the legacies of our forefathers
that has been stolen
& together we're rolling
to regain our lost estate...
many are called, but few are chosen
and we are the few that's beholding...
respect that's due.
Respect that hue... man...

In human form we are God bodies...
short, tall, skinny, fat, hard cocky
property of the most high
that keeps a close eye
on reasons why I spit...
I spit to reach y'all, greet y'all, and teach y'all
what you need to hear.
All you need is one ear,
one eye & one tear
to feel this shhh like it needs to be felt
and succeed in ya steps
to greatness.
This is REAL TALK we put veils on fakeness.
We spreading LOVE like Bob Marley,
so how can you hate this!?
What a line up...
This is divine stuff
that'll turn your brain to water...
We broke up the iron cuffs
and crumbled the shackles...
Such a humbled spectacle
when we are looked at
prison changed us.
We gave the title crook back...
Gave the killer back...
Gave the thug back...
us being victims of RECIDIVISM,
the prison system
will love that.
I know my true purpose in life now... Let me rub that,
I am Short just in case you're wondering who's this dude...
An upright Moor that's on his square like a Rubik's cube
I spit for humanity!!!

Spit With a Purpose...

What's the essence of Man...knowledge!
Whether he obtain it or not.
The plot was,
infinite intelligence
the relevance is cosmic elements,
college is the evidence.
You're a university, a unit universally
my verses be,
of the universe times 33.
A degree—from the tiniest light,
I write from a molecular level of life,
then burn 7 trillion sun masses bright from left to right.
I can't recite individual realities,
those fallacies are
minute perspectives living third planet from the Sun---god;
Amon—Ra!
I'm visiting the third galaxies from area 51.
I fit the one...son...god...Malik?
One God is Yah!
My mobility is speed of thought, thought it was psychic,
let us write this in our image and likeness,
without truth man is lifeless...
And lifelessness is destructive... Counterproductive.
The seven layers of skin is within the terrestrial structure.
I'm an extra celestial conundrum
could none sum, my existence?
Bore both genesis and exodus before human resistance,
can't compute the ethnic war plight.
---senseless how sections' for fight.
My foresight is star gates and wormholes.
I Spit With a Purpose to burn holes through mental circuits,
never seen the surface!
I cipher with subcultures,
on subconscious frequencies in
subterranean mainframes fleeing word poachers
this world is full of vultures.

I keep my truth to my chest,
I'm alien like that.
Obscured trinities asked me how I move like that.
I'm O.N.E.-N.E.O-FOR AN E.O.N.
I'm definite.. and science have no end.
I advance man's technology.
Complexity's stellar trigonometry.
-follow me the complete distance of men,
move in angles the average angels among us
can't get in...
I can't get out.
I'm a devout movement about homo sapiens,
became educated to reform the deform shape we in
I exercise mind muscles, produce uncanonized scribes,
I'm an apocrypha;
a poetic apocalypse devised to spit,
universally in any galaxy with diversity...
On any planet, in any language
with any species that seek me,
you could reach me
in Alpha Centauri if the need be!!!

Spit With a Purpose...

Specifically for the species of specimen,
sub and extraterrainians,
unconscious and conscious
of their cosmic and chromatic connections.
Whose cries are concepts,
which lie concealed deep in cerebral caverns,
with life lessons and levels like labyrinths.
Uncommunicated---
Cause common conduit earlobes
can't log on or carry the load of the complex.
Light year leaping language
of the arcane architects and recluse hierophants.
Who reside in the recesses
of the systematic seat control called sol.
Construction the unconversated
like creating stargazers,
by causing constellations to converge
within the eyes of the queen sex.
Same said as the suicide strains
that flow through the veins of the other world outcast who don't feel
they belong.
So they desire to move on to the next plane,
and thus deal damage to they mainframes.
I spit this!
Precisely to puncture the 6 chakras
and physical preceptors,
which stumblingly stitched simplistic science
to finance and propagate fictitious phenomenon.
Which paralyzed the people like a poison potion.
Pushing them to pelt out pitiful pleas called prayers
goat scaping sent through forest
packed with cares.
Which made them called they power-less.
I spit to awake Ken neurons
and fine tune tone static stagnated frequencies,
to become receptive to realms and wormholes.

Where minds can move as moles,
traveling beyond clocks of mach speed,
for those that don't know matters can be anti and energy so high it can
defy
Polarity.
Allotting the great optic observation
in the cavity of zero gravity.
I hawk symphonies of Bach
to bring back ingrained pain
felt in humane frames
in forms of soul bared bars
as if I shed tears sitting upon mars to get a visual, picture imploding stars.
I spit to asphyxiate
astro-nots who need aids
to space out the span-Ce of lines.
Laced with land minds
cause fear is life's inhibitors
so welcome the invaders evolved
breachers of your parameters.
We the A-liens!
Those who seek your extinction so you can live
morphers of your mental make up
to once again be aquatic.
So you can survive and thrive
in this saliva of the astral attic.
I spit to cause you pause
and levitate your lexicon
the very selection in the number 8 position I spit
is to warn you we came to conquer not co-exist
and build you to breathe.
Nurturing nebulous nectar
from the physical universe called brain vector.
We have arrived first words of the
invading 8th sector.

Spit With a Purpose...

Although I Spit With a Purpose,
sometimes I spit propaganda,
like a radical cleric
with an anti-American agenda.
I birth movements
leave society to remove the placenta.
My ego bent with a slant,
I ain't got a soul,
I got a poltergeist who loves to rant.
And he presents to you
these literary Rembrandts.
And you can seek pleasure
like Bohenian rejects.
Chasing after Bermuda
sunsets.
I spit profound obscenities
like a wise man with
tourettes.
My words-Tarantulas
in this universal web of design.
Went to bed with Solomon's
concubines.
Broke bread with Wisdom
and fathered Sunshine.
Let there be light.
Now,
let there be a
lookalike.
Call it a hologram or a prototype.
I proliferate poems with protoplasm,
touch enough erogenous zones
to give angels an orgasm,
my organs more unholy than phantasm.
Let's eliminate the formalities,
I believe in one God with a split-personality.
I split Atoms like

Schrodinger
and call it intellectual brutality.
You can't clone my physicality.
To all you astrophysicists trying to defy
gravity,
I give you a face lift
so you can face this mental blizzard
and catch my snow drifts.
I mean—my chemical snow bliss.
My words plague young minds
like Egyptian locusts.
Probably find me sitting in a Tibetan cave
sitting full lotus.
Intergalactic cops
tried to arrest me on Planet Earth
for impersonating Seven Seraphim's
In seven parallel universes.
Implement life in my verses.
Bend light with a mental force
that's coercive.
Telepathy of an earthling,
unearth the mystery of
Atlantis; city lost.
The tears I shed is for the holocaust.
I ain't talking about Germany.
I'm talking about
Transatlantic.
Take a Pan am to C16 planet.
Don't ask why I spit,
or why I sound pissed.
You should be asking God
how to understand my
Bullshit.

SPIT WITH A PURPOSE...

My theory of flows delivering information
to souljahs brain cells—
poetically liberating stem cells---
concrete walls bringing a generation to a pause!
Open paragraphs got scholars applauding;
at my secrete teaching of life---
Studying ancient Judaism, got me.
Spitting; With a Purpose like "Nas"
close my third eye, I'm able to see life on Mars---
Lyrics lyrically so biblically,
resurrecting the bible characteristically
in Out Creye the Rebirth,
giving voice to universal Kings!
Personal parables penetrating genetic codes,
impregnated Isis and produced Egyptian Queens!
Recorded sounds of physics in ink
predicating destiny with every blink---
Holding deep conversations with Gabriel in my sleep
exchanged blueprints to baptize bastards,
politicians speaking non-English!
I execute matrix tactics
strapped with a sword type pen,
my African jewels burst into atomic numbers---
once consumed causing typhoons
for those who use my Holy name in vain---
I'm a Son of a God "Sun" Godson of a prophet, Ahmose!
Congregating at the Towers of Out Creye (2)
searching for a synagogue to go pray into—
Wondering why Bush didn't
send telegraphs
to hit institutional gun
towers, towering over our youth?!
Sideline troops dressed in Nazi suits!
And they wonder why I'm so spiritual!!
Forgive me Yah!
But my metaphors defecating on microphones

how sista Lauren Hill do---
It's true,
"mis-education of a black woman" I miss you too!
You made contact with my super-conscious
while meditating in the safari
and made a love poem that made Medusa, feel beautiful!
Style compared to magical music
turning disbelievers into dust.
Syllables vandalized abandoned mental's;
Brainstorming with Revolutionary talking eternity Revolution-
Reverse my physical birth---
Speeding as a sperm, striving to become existence
twisting forever more in the flesh,
seeking for stable substance---
"I was at peace!"
Now, I'm chosen to be immortalized,
dethroned from a place where there's no pulse
arteries and skeletons are futuristic-
reborn through an invisible time zone,
resurrected through death is how I'm told to return home---
Born into a world that's never been awaken,
surrounded by natural disasters that has this earth shaken-
Heard this is only for a season! Searching my spiritual beliefs
trying to compound these reasons!
Wrote 21St century telescope for our history! Learned wisdom
from Machiavelli Tha Don that'll have this nation shocked—
Watching the star's struggling to hear the "tic toc" on life
time; as I watch—"tic toc, is the sound"... Tic toc.

The warm up

SPIT WITH A PURPOSE...

The reason I spit!
This was an open invite but I wasn't expected to show,
I've heard them, so now I'm answering prayers and snatchin' halos.
Coming right and exact, truth equality be born square.
Follow this mental message close and awake from the nightmare.
Asked could I spit with a purpose, so purposely I spit.
Shine light on the B.S. to eliminate the bull shhh, that's it.
I do this for the young stars; I do this for the hoods
I do it for the bad and all of that's to the good.
On the rise empowerment to the people to give birth to God's nation
Happy birthday to the Black stars that hungers for a strong foundation
From the most high they get fed, and lovin' what they're tastin'
All original and civilized people approved with no more time wasted.
See this as a quick fix
A lesson against politrick's
No political science degree is necessary, when you're a born scientist
Peace to the true and living deeply rooted in the laws of nature
giving sight to the blind. Who've been mislead by false saviors.
I self lord am master; always masterly stand on my L seven.
LOVE GOD arise from the depths of hell and seat yourself in heaven.
Self eradication eradicating that self destructive boogie man.
Leave six for the crucifix and travel twenty three million of useful land.
From the mountain top I hale
In the hereafter I prevail
Love, protect, and respect our earths And be positive **Black males**!
Know that our young seeds.
Do follow close to our leads
Keep the knowledge add on cipher right and be an open book to read.
Understand that it's positive elevation above corrupt evolution
Meaning be careful what you teach and be ready for revolution
Be direct in your approach and be lead to the correct conclusions.
Everybody has complaints,
but who gonna come with the solutions.
This is the reason I spit; for way more than one purpose.
If I sell out I get the hell out what I spit is not for purchase.
If I have to sell it my words become worthless.

The reason I spit now, is because it's best if the world heard this...

SPIT WITH A PURPOSE...

I'm so over the rhetoric
this ova rhetorical climate
is what's causing my oral oracles to climax.
I spit **D**epleted, **N**eurotic, **A**toms,
into cranial cavities.
When my vocabulary semen-
I seed men who be acting over dramatic,
unconscious and unresponsive-
My reaction becomes---anti prophylactic,
meaning,
my verse is prolific when it ejaculate.
I'm one---solar entity
whose mental extremities are extremely bi-
My thoughts are out the closet.
I spit from atop Twin Towers that terrorist can't target
Medulla---Oblongata!
My insights are Cyclops
I binocular my third eye,
to bifocal the micro.
I write cryptic poetry in corn crops.
my messianic prose entertain Scarecrows,
in this field of art,
harvesting the brain dead, brain cells-
I'm the Wizard of Oxymoron's!
My neurons are corn fed-
I laid in bed with my super Id,
only to give birth to an alter ego-
I'm intellectually inbred,
my thoughts are next akin-
I spit from lips too suave to swab,
my saliva test positive for incest,
I spit with cerebral palsy-
My omnipotence is bipartisan
I'm the spitting image of ABBA Father.
Spitting isms skillfully enough to homo-erect-us
not just the young and restless.

My exorcist is ambidextrous
somewhat dyslexic,
especially when my tourette spit.
I sit King with the likes of Supreme men
Pros and Cons who've returned to the ONE-
I AM...
Alphabetically Alpha!
That's the STATE of mind I'm in
CITY men call me COUNTRY
but consciously,
my vowels and consonants be CONTINENTS!
I know that my vernacular is as unnatural as
imported Indian hair sported by Africans-
but with it I support my people
like picks with the black fist uplift afros.
My blackness resemble black holes-
Earth bored,
too deep for Tiger Woods to birdie-
I'm batty when my attic is disturbed
and well versed to suck the blood out the vain-
My word game got fangs-
I'm the Black Dracula...
And my ego is submissive like Egor-
I spit to knock chips off shoulders of poets
to make them eager for more.
Social
Problems
Intellectually
Translated
With a Purpose!
I spit to serve you,
or I can spit to <u>serve you</u>!
If ever you vex the vegetation of my
inner vegetarian.
My Good Samaritan may crave meat-
I can spit **Project Parables** to the meek
and make obese the anorexia of my humanitarian,
or I can eat,

then defecate on paper,
My dispensation stank-
I'm the shhh!
I spit to keep the ball moving
like bowels-
And I run with some wild-wild spitters from Chi-town
that spit like diarrhea-
We the realist!
The line up---
We knitted tight like the quilt of Linus-
I'mma Spit With a Purpose,
until we find us.

Art by Zelle

In Loving Memory of

Carmen Cannon

Black Rose

Chapter one

BLACK ROSE

I cried like a child with colic, when the word came that the Word sent word to his Angels saying; "deliver these wings to the most beautiful woman I've ever created."

Confused and dazed, and though I understand God ways and the meaning and seasons concerning planting and reaping, still it's hard for me to reasonably reason with the reasons why he chose to harvest the "Eve" of this Golden Garden. SHE WAS MY EDEN!...a black rose that the creator sowed and told to be fruitful and grow...and she did! though her ground wasn't tilled or fallow, somehow every meadow, pasture and landscape she walked became hallowed, and with wide open nostrils I followed the aroma of her floristic flower, and like pheromones! I chased the sweet nectar of her nurturing pollens,

"but still I cry for her blossoms."

Her phenom won't leave me alone. And the hiss of my entombed monotone sass its sad song through my brass soul like an un—tuned saxophone, belligerently bellowing its melodramatic antics and emotional tantrums, screaming, "YOUR GONE TOO SOON!"

I'm losing my sanity, and my moodiness moves me to blasphemy, so I'm shaking my fist towards Heaven wondering why its host didn't bail yelling Geronimo!!! when she was quacking, heart racing, fading....comatose!

Ashamed, the Moon moved beyond its place and the Sun refrained its rays, now I'm living in shades of grey feeling all blue in the face. And as I sashay through this purple haze, I can't help but ask the question:

"what was it that ailed you?"

Why didn't you tell me that there was a thorn in your side! Lord know's I would've abandoned my pride and took strides to pry at your aches and crowbar your pain until it became ajar. Or maybe I could've sent my words in the form of pesticides unharmful to you, but armed with enough accolades to ostracize that prickly thicket that choked the life out of you.

Forgive me for painting a picture so damn vivid-----this is my pain speaking.

See, my memories of you are still pictures, still wet and dripping with pigments of your beauty; duty calls me to reshape our history and calibrate the tilted frame that bezel these memories.

Remember when our smiles collaborated and collided like abstract collages. Vibrant displays of love spray-painted and brush stroked on the canvas we unraveled.

My soul is forever tatted with the graffiti graphics of your soft fingerprints, and my heart bleeds with the hues of your finger-paints that drip like sweat from your ceramic fingertips, truly, you are a
"MASTERPIECE!"

Black Rose, your smile is the one wonder my mind humbly savor, besides the diamond glints that burst from your eyes like dancing flames, these are the sparks you create, sparks that ignite arid hearts.

I remember the squint in your eyes and how they would become sunrises when your heart bade to say something, Lord, why did her sunset have to come so quick!

did you really have to take her in a twinkling of an eye? for goodness sake! was it for the twinkle in her eyes?

I stand here cold, un-consoled, trying to define the meaning of my visible breath, I'm steaming with anger, yet painstakingly freezing.

Carmen, all I have left is your rose petals, Chauncey, Love and Tay, and I promise to cherish them as I have cherished you, wholeheartedly and unconditionally,

Endlessly, I will forever water the memory of your existence with every tear within me, so that the essence of your beauty with grow
"infinitely"

In loving memory of my dear friend
Carmen Cannon,
My Black Rose

The Marriage

I'm just a man
a mere mortal, a spirit abnormal
the soul of the creation
the earth' s first generation.
Birthed from water like 7 continental nations,
not a drop wasted from the Sun's ejaculation,
and the Motherland's immaculate conception
was a physical demonstration.
Yet I felt her contractions underneath my feet
that's how deep this thing had my heart racing.
Can't say that I witnessed the first 5 creations.
I was born on the 6 day and I was all by myself...
on this great big rock,
cried to Yah all by myself, palms open like
why you give me this heart to be hopeless.
And my prayers were pried from brokeness
provoking this being...this thing...this extreme
strenuousness to pull on the fabric of my existence,
string by string.
Cling to the plot shriveling meekly inside this story,
for mine eyes have seen the glory,
looking into the firmament hoping that this openness
in the pit of my stomach won't destroy me.
Regurgitated emotions from Heaven heavily toy
with me!!! -boy it's me!!!
the voice sound familiar...
feel like I been knowing you all my life, like
I'm married to this feeling
and this feeling my wife.
I laid with her and she conceived.
I imagine the blessings I receive...
2 seeds-10 fold-a new breed-better believe me.
I was given to greed, from the very first kiss.
Changed the whole damn creed, and I fell
victim to her bliss.
Be careful not to misjudge this.

But we were naked in the crib before she clothed me,
see, I sacrificed more than a rib -she exposed me-
and I paid for that dearly -you hear me-
I love her sincerely
so -seriously that I shed the old me curiously.
To see what that do to me.
She was new to me and she grew to me,
flew to me like a dove from the Heaven above
down on my shoulder -it was over
cuzz, she truly drew me from the madness
that consumed me.
Ruined me in the process but we were one flesh
and Yah blessed me with her for me.
For my sake and I shake at the thought
of her being taken from me to be given back to me
so that we can be complete...that's a hell of a feat.
Knowledge is deep and she is my love, my life, my wife,
my soul she keep.
I'm in love with knowledge
as she protects me from me.

THE AMERICA YOU HELP START

Dear Mister One Dollar, President George Washington,
you are the embodiment of Pandora's box and dejection
breathing oxygen as you travel in many directions
until fives, tens and twenties intersect, and
fifties and hundreds connect and will into subjection, but still,
let's just take you away from the collection of bills
and hand you over to the ills of life
so you can see the chills of strife.
The bank teller held you tight, and
she was just trying to do good.
But the bank robber held a knife, and
you was his livelihood. So he killed her right where she stood,
snatched you away and ran to the hood
spent you on drugs after being down a dollar-
short for a slug, but now he got you to give to the thug,
who accepts you despite being smudged with innocent blood.
No second thought, he just gives it a shrug
because he know Ladybug in that strip club be dancing for studs
owning to the fact that she got to feed food to her cubs,
so in exchange for you, she's willing to accept some rubs.
Show dude some love, and even though dude's nasty,
she gives him a hug.
He gives her you, but she was expecting a dub.
She calls him a scrub and put her bra back on her jugs and leave.
She goes home to a daughter begging her:
"please I want some ice cream mommy!"
So she gives you away.
Her daughter takes you in order to pay the ice cream truck.
It would've been a nice thing but
across the street was a shorty only nineteen
looking for a fast buck, and now you have another low class nut
who felt like he was down on his last luck.
So with the gun that he had clutched,
he quickly dashed to the truck
like a snake when the grass is cut
and told the man inside to give the cash up.

The man refused, so shorty was fast to bust.
And guess who the blast struck, Mr. President, U.S. Figurehead.
The stripper's daughter ended up dead. Shorty fled
but not before grabbing the creation of the fed.
He picked you up and ran straight ahead
to escape the cop car flashing blue and red, but
with a three block perimeter spread, police popped him
something like a blackhead, and now
inside the evidence room, Mister Capital Bread,
you waiting single and lonely for that armor truck to pony you
home free to where them loans be handed out wrongly
by executive phonies who control you and billions of your currency
cronies,
and they know some clones be up in the fold
because America don't hold that much gold.
So it's all a trick.
Counterfeit money made in part to benefit those leaders in charge.
Culprits without love in their hearts for the America you help start,
Mr. President, one dollar Czar. This is a grave ordeal,
and what's bizarre
is not the people that steal
but the ones that don't mark you to see if your real.

THE BEST RAPPER ALIVE
(J-HOVA!)

He never went platinum
even though he packed plateaus and platforms
and moved crowds with no microphone.
He was a phenom in rare form,
who caused palms to wave side to side when his hype-man
hyped fanatics with hypercritical hymns rendering them hyperactive
and some even hypocritical.
His metaphysical flow performed miracles,
literally,
his deliverance had the lyrical ability to touch the lame,
he was a ill dude,
performed Beatitudes to multitudes,
telling them "I Love You" before them Beatle dudes.
He chanced the road when he turned 12,
left footprints in the sand.
He became scholar when he kicked knowledge to his colleagues,
he was head strong.
Started writing songs when he came upon an adulteress in distress,
heard chants of Jazebel! hailed
from a band of men bearing stones,
over zealots,
jealous because she chose to bear her neo-soul.
J-Hova battled for her soul,
wrote a deep poem on the ground,
so deep that rap went underground.
No more accusers around so,
he began touring towns in search of b-boys to be down for his label.
Found 12 and named them Apostles,
taught them how to cipher with righteous thoughts
and how to be devout.
See, in this region there's other b-boys called legion,
who sell out seats in a club called "Synagogue"
where these pretenders plagiarize the song "Genesis"
that J-Hova wrote in the beginning when he was still with the trinity.
He was always about his father's business,

but this was personal,
so on purpose he overturned tables in his anger,
thus coining the term, "Turn-Tables."
But the timetable for DJ's was still years away,
so the crowd became pagan.
That's when "Death Row" became a label.
They wanted to battle the Apostles with two rappers
who's free-styles was savage,
so savage they'll torched dudes on the Sabbath,
so they called them, Sodom and Gomorrah
who put the cables on a perverse generation.
They began to rake money in,
went from 50¢ to a million pence.
That was the "Aftermath.
J-Hova was the brand, so he became the "Rock"
Took one off the team cause he booked 30 talents behind his back
and crooked what was right.
Later that night, a group called, "Sanhedrin"
found J-Hova in the garden of Gethsemane, resting,
the rest of his crew too,
when Judas came through and boosted the masters
to J-Hova's music.
That was the beginning of Gangster Rap,
the day that **N**iggas **W**ith **A**ttitudes plotted on his debut album,
called, "The Second Adam"
Herod who managed "Death Row" for Caiaphas
brought J-Hova before his kangaroo court,
and the Jews who owned this sport,
openly scourged his butt.
He never said much, he was old school,
only spoke when spoken to.
But when they pushed the vote through,
it was over for J-Hova,
at least that's what they told 'em.
But here's the tyranny,
the soldier who speared him in the back
sold his masters to a white rapper
who dropped his first album and went platinum.

Them dirty bastards!
J-Hova never went platinum,
all because his brawn was bronze and wool,
so they put 'em on the wood.

And it seemed as if things stood at a stalemate,
especially after his plea,
"My God, my God, why have you forsaken me?"
He battled the lyrical temptations of the Satan emcee
who spoke ether with a sinister tone.
The dis was so bad,
his own people mocked his throne.
But J-Hova knew he was King all along.
Henceforth, similar to the album "Kingdom Come"
with the single "Lost One"
but for many souls.
They destroyed his temple,
but he rebuilt it in three days
because he was the Blueprint.
He tried to tell the world he was boss,
but they had no faith-
just Reasonable Doubt and corrupted thoughts.
And now, he's worth more than other rappers
and not in earthly cost.
Before Makaveli,
he hung on a cross.

HELLO

Excuse me miss,
at the risk of comin' off chauvinistic,
I was listenin' to that switch in ya hips & couldn't resist it.
That's just a joke, you know, to cope wit the tension.
My hope is to open a "convo" to commence with.
Also on my list is for us to just kick it
have a real talk without sayin "real talk" in it.
You look like you like when I look, I'm just guess in'
you had me in mind when you outlined your selection.
The walk you walkin', the smile that you givin',
I feel like your mission was to get my attention.
Well you got it, now you can get my intentions
& we can lay the base to start our ascension.
But lemme start simple, just talk wit you
your physical makin' me want to know your mental.
I want to get in touch wit you emotional too,
& I didn't buy you a drink because I want the sober you.
Simply said, I see my future in you
if this is the start of that, I want it to continue.
I got jewelry, but the jewels I share ain't diamonds
just cuz it glitter it ain't gold cuz it's shinin'.
My thinkin' is the thinkin' of a man with a new swag
& that man should provide you wit more than just a new bag.
Money ain't the place where you base a relationship
the basics say the basis is the love you placin' in it.
& I got my half if you willin' to take it in
You ain't gotta answer now I just want you to take it in
& weigh the weight of how serious the things I'm sayin' is.
I wanna be the reason of your complacency
& you to be the last tenant in my heart's vacancy.
I got destiny tellin' me that I need you next to me,
forget the waffle house I need a soul food recipe.
The same one "Big Mama" laid on "Grandpop"
this is the day that my'one night stands stop.
If you wit it, I want more than a quick cut

I see more in you than a "pretty face & big butt"
Everything I'm sayin' is the truth heartfelt
but before I'm all in maybe I should introduce myself.

I WONDER WHAT AWAITS ME...!

When the gates swing open & the mother of life embraces me.

Will an orchestra of birds serenade me with a chorus conducted by the
wings of a
butterfly.

Or maybe the sky will applaud my arrival with thunderous roars as its
native son returns
home to reclaim his rightful place.

I imagine in a meditative state, the clouds parting as the Sun wraps its
warmth around my
face.

I can even envision the smile of my Mother piercing through the heavens
as two rain
drops sprinkle my face with her tears & even as anticipation morphs the
fear, I can feel the
protective hand of my father & hear his whispering voice calmly speaking
"Son I'm still here!"

I dream at times, walking into the out stretched hands of my life saver.

Often times staying in that mind frame, savoring every image
photographed in that mind
frame.

Still I wonder what awaits me, when my feet touch the concrete &
freedom shakes my
hand!

Will squirrels , gather in amazement watching as the Universe bestow
upon me the riches from Gods tomb & with the blessing of the cosmos
congratulate my arrival with the unveiling of my First Lady.

Resembling the grace & integrity of the First Lady, then our First Baby will be the first baby & if all goes well, we'll name our Son Barack or our Daughter Michelle.

Completing destiny's trail while laying the foundation for the road ahead.

Unable to take a glance into the unknown, I wonder if the hovering spotlight will
accentuate the poetic prowess of the king as I embed my footprints in the blueprints used
to construct my stage & If M.J. shot phrases, it'll be me he'll have to battle for title of all
time greatest.

I anticipate erecting my own monument. Uniting centers with the monumental
"Spitting with a Purpose" that I dispense.

I look forward to doing community service not handed down by the courts. I'm talking
about serving the community & keeping my lil' brothers & sisters from being statistics
of them.

Maybe if I service them right, they can be the Judges& Lawyers redefining our position
in this fight.

I predict this and more from where I stand. Where I once sat idle, I stand engaged.
Vigorously diligent in pursuit of what's for me.

I understand that I do control what I control & as I wander, I still wonder, what awaits
me.

Home From War

If beauty was in the eye of the beholder
what then is in the grasp of the soldier
who trugged through time when colder huh?
for better for worst was first
from kiss on the cheek to between the sheets
now got to kiss cheeks just so she uh speak
the fight for the life of love goes on deep
in the trenches of the skeet
where real men really show what they do for bread and meat
so baby and little lady can eat
nobody hears him though
when the cry for crime let go
echo
as the wind blow tried to shovel but had to push snow
and when terrain changed had to make change
so plucking puffing and
pushing weed was a demand where he supplied needs
all this for living, loving and surviving
and for this hard work he should be driving
Mercedes or Lexus
not a blue bird headed for Texas
but the law of life is not justice
it's just this
when a man is on the battle field of love
then there's the place where he better be ready to die cuz
no matter how many metals or
material things he may bring home
the joy won't last long
cuz like the Country he's fighting to keep on
if she loved him he wouldn't have had to be gone
what now is in the soldiers grasp
you asked his heart dignity and identity
cuz the beauty is actually ugly and his once love is his enemy.

TEAR DROPS

Pure pressure from a tiers terrace
is pure terror.
temperatures swelters to the degree that melt thermometers
and climb like vines in Celsius.
The atmosphere so dense that my infrared senses can't heat seek
there's no barometer pressure.
I'm sweating bullets----bloodletting!
I feel as though my motor skills need to let some steam off
so like tears I'ma squeeze off a few shell casing
face it, I'm ballistic
and you can trace my insanity back like shell casings.
My eyes are bloodshot red that shed and leave traces like
munition tracers.
I'm seeing double through the scope of a single shot triple beam
I gotta get the mote out.
Hear my soul cry out.
I'ma wolf without a pack with a raspy howl
and my canines are broken into sound bites
so now I converse through open muzzles like spoken words
combust through open mics-
A mutha f-cka gone heed my bark til my barrel turns hoarse
full moon or not-
I'm terrible like Czar
and bananas when my kalashnikov roar like Tarzan and Boy.
Get my narrative!
Pain....I'm married to it
plus Mary Jane got my mind blown....bliss!
yeah I'm smoking
eyes so low it's like the window of opportunity is closing
but I'm a opportunist who powers forward
a sharpshooter like Ray Allen---a power forward
whose perimeter shot is similar to the invisible bullet that killed Kennedy.
Damn---I gotta control my breathing-
I'm about to make it rain, mist even.
I'm on a mission
and my target is the park opposite this building

where plenty pedestrians flock like pilgrims on Plymouth-
this gone be a turkey shoot
but before I drop this shot like Turkoglu
I wanna give Thanksgiving.
Times are grim and I'm hungry
so I'm fed signs and omens that read shoot to kill.
I can't seem to breathe up here
the air is too thin for my lungs capacity
as if the wind done lost weight
and it's crazy how these paper thin clouds done lost shade-
I'm exposed
unspoken but ready to shoot the breeze literally-
you can hear my anger in the wind----whistling.
Life is cold and I'm shivering in it,
the elements got me rapped in misery,
I can't weather it.
I'm wide open,
like the rat sized hole my rifle nose is poking out of,
I'ma let it blow like nostrils
and fo sho gone close somebody's curtain,
and if not fo sho, then fo certain.
I'ma a man hurting, whose feet are sore from soul searching,
the show is over,
no encores, just elbows and assholes,
ambulances and hearses accessing the damage,
Damn it!
she shouldn't have left me,
mama told me life was a bitch,
now because of this bitch I'm about to suffocate humanity,
you catch my drift, ain't nobody safe,
I'm about to commit murder by asphyxiation and
catch a pillow case.
This is the American way,
to dialect thru any means, well I prefer a mini 14,
that'll bring forth screams.
Nature is silenced like asylums,
and birds can't sing over sirens.
This ain't rumors of wars,

my rifle can't wait to gossip like lou
in lieu of a bent soul,
I'm Iffel like that tower over in Pisa, I'm bent over,
and I ain't talking submission,
I'm in attack mode.
Damn! I gotta control my breathing,
I gotta control these demons,
and I got a legion in this extra clip,
and I'm about to heeve them, hail them even
like bats outta hell,
let'em rip, these fears, when I wet my peers.
Pure pressure perpetuated from a tiers terrace
is pure terror.
But I ain't no terrorist
so I'ma let these tears drop instead.

Overhead from the tier top
my tear drops fall and crush into the pavement
and transform into diamonds.
the clarity clearly made me aware of the jewel I really lost.
My view point was really off,
but it's too late to turn back with strife.
My eye in the scope and I'm preying on the circle of life.
I 7-20 with a 30 yard 60,
which means I three sixty the scenery twice.
Prob massacre.
Muhammad nor Manson
could mastermind the madness I mapped in my deer rack.
I promise to bring life hell,
and I wish one death for one who wishes one well.
Malvo in the keyhole.
I breathe slow
and step to that line and end a nigga game like a free throw.
Final score is my .223 to life's zero.
Pure terror.
Tales of a terrorist who tears can be traced back to conception.
Screw life perception.
No exceptions.

Keep your kids in the house because collateral damage is expected.
They're going to follow my shell casings and drop tears forever.
For years ran suicide drills with Blue Devils.
It's evident, no rhetoric.
My shot magic like J.J. Reddick sh-t.
Beyond stress.
Plus my pain different
unknown like the variable X.
I see the sun black and wish the world death
DEAD!
but I'm no terrorist,
so I'm going to let these tear drops fall instead.

POTENTIAL

As the nights creep away she's awaken by the Sun's sprinkles through the
curtain,
No alarm clock just a heart of someone that's determined,
As she (sits) and meditates on the days scheduled event,
She skillfully plans her every move, better than her yesterday,
Motivated from her visions of being in a better place,
Not letting her circumstances confine her destiny,
So she's focused on surpassing life's misery,
She's educated from politics to science,
Captivated by histories defiance,
Yet liberated with prestigious alliance,
Perfecting her weakness, still aware of her spiritual strengths
Secure in any element and will go great lengths,
Contend until there's no one left,
Content only with success,
I'm elated as I hear such credentials,
Left speechless as she passes by,
She's Potential!.

The Wailing Wall

Let's go to Eden
where Eve's eating
apples, Adam tackled
with thoughts of a beating.
behind bushes retreating.
Moses led us out of Egypt
and into the desert. We flipped.
Nothing but sand to sip.
The cost of the promise land
was an ego trip.
I'm hearing bars rattle and clink
we back in Pharaoh's precinct.
My ghetto instinct refuses to blink.
Incarceration of the youth-
Systematic design, what you think?
Inquisition of the Moors, Spanish alliance
an army of mannish lions, fierced and unmanaged
banished to Ethiopia's gates where swords are brandished.
Bruised and bandaged, abused collateral damage.
Psychological famished
sandwiched in between
Mr. I have a dream
and
brother by any means.
Growth stinted by a sentence
replenished under the bented
authority of Judges of slavery
my heart pumps Nat Turners bravery
ask Afeni only God can judge me
life goes on, I ain't mad at cha
for not loving me
If he was alive, intellectually
I'm where Machiavelli would be
seven days of Godfather trilogy
bullets ricochet
this is no ordinary love similar to Sade.

Our addictions is slavery
habitual tendencies, alcohol and Hennessey
asking my ego who's the enemy
he didn't respond tentatively
he screamed, "you see what they did to Kennedy!"
Put a hole in his memory
remember me
I'm spitting voraciously
from plantations to penitentiary plants
It's like we in concentration camps
(they came before Columbus, but my great-great grandfather
come on a slave ship named Jesus. Across the Atlantic Ocean
chained to the insane notion you can judge men by the
color of their skin. Put down your crayons. Color doesn't
exist. We invented it. Philosophical puzzles. Different shades
of light reflects what we see. Bottom line-they gone respect
you and me.)
Second temple of Jerusalem
Solomon's in the veins
I was ordained
to spit vicious and sick
a twisted dimwit
social misfit, mental conniptions of a lunatic
herded like Jews and sent to slaughter
holocaust of our African sons and daughters
Mussolini laughing from the graveyard
war of the worlds, Y2K, swim in Iraq tears
towers collapsed, bones found on ground zero
CIA plotting to make Bin Laden a hero
murdered and martyred
the truth deserted and bartered
so berserk it hurts, trapped on earth
we bend blocks, our future is cemetery dirt
shining with jewelry
cops putting cases on us with a fury
my name stated for the jury
predicated offenses, black on black crime
statistics and chalk lines

premeditated signs of pregnant teens crying
absentee fathers
low-life boys who didn't want to be bothered
destruction of Pearl Harbor
strapped with TNT, reality TV
retaliated for Waco like Timothy McVeigh
the people's temple of Jim Jones
we the people,
believe in the right to be massacred.
Let our family grieve
at the Wailing Wall.

STAR CHILD

The requisition of chauvinistic rhetoric implies, a man's first born
should come in the form of a son,
    and I agree that it make sense in the sense that a son is the pedigree
and stock of a man's strength, but what men tend to omit, is that
spiritually we were light, years before we were born flesh,
    so, in retrospect of translucentness,
"She is, my SUN…"

Her manifestation of scintillation was created because I eclipsed the
Moons gravishere, without fear, fearlessly penetrating the circumference
of its radiance.
    I illuminated her incandescence under the cover of darkness as we
conjugated in conjugal consummation for hours without confrontation.
    I sparked the ovulation of her outer limits, stimulating the elation of
her luster, clusters of capricious blithe shimmered brilliantly and in its
brilliance, she became resilient,
    her brilliance gave birth when my energy touched the realm of her
Earths virginity, giving life to seven spectrums of light,
    Red, Orange, Yellow, Green, Blue, Indigo and Violet prisms,
engendered brightness retained in her retinas and irises, biologically,
    all because I wooed the Moon into submission when my fingertips
made its landing, sending chills through her satellite intervals, causing
sensations where no atmosphere has been before.

Moonstruck,
I painstakingly explored her curvaceous surface, caressing the
contrast of her sweat filled craters,
    later, we revolved in a slightly elliptical orbit, making love while
weathering nuclear shower storms, and in our resolve, we evolved,
    bringing the light to fruition through spherical bliss,
the luminosity of a,
"Star Child…"

Kuta

Breaking News!

This is psychological war agenda
Intel ain't wholesale, it's retail
And inflation high, but quality of information low
So the price to pay is high risk,
when the news weak its credit is bad
This is financial, mental beneficial report
The news!
Is equivalent to your brain on medication
A story stimulant broadcasted to keep your sense sedated
We need news rehab;
It is a reason to why the revolution won't be televised
Its propaganda is ill advised and need to be revived
Our world view is hooked to a picture tube,
we're remotely wired for change
It's a war of words, for control of the population
underlying homeland security-
Their top-story is hearsay and the bottom line is gossip
And inquiring minds seeks garbage, so magazines profit
It's a bomb brigade bombarding your common sense with sensors
Breaking news!
This just in, kid killers on a rampage
It was pressed and printed on front page
The police profile led to public outrage
Three black teens placed in peril
The prosecutor said the pistol had no prints, and teens no priors
But the pressure to prosecute led to a preliminary hearing
The grand jury indicted because it was under false pretense-
Breaking news!
It's more than stereotypical views, it's your mind being tainted
your life being swayed, your emotions being played
The mind is fragile, and information heavy
This is a broadcast alert!

Men

My life ain't never been normal,
so these harsh circumstances only mean that I'm livin'
I could be, more formal and perform like a gentleman
disguising my greed but hey, I'm a wolf like Robin Givens.
I'm out to get it, whether Spoken Words or
when words spoken, I'm provokin' emotions.
My words are smokin' and you can actually
see them leavin' my lips when my mouth is open.
Look; I'm a hypothetical thought translated
in literal terms to propound theological doctrines
that divides human beings.
To be Christ-like
would be preposterous if we really perceive biblical things.
Scriptures strip us of what's said
and what it really means.
Theoretically it's great but,
we would pass out before the first nail puncture
flesh as we die in our screams.
So I can, only be me-like and ask Yahweh
to have mercy on my soul before I depart,
I ain't no Angel, no Matthew or no Mark,
a sinner maybe that's just what my Aunt said
and she said she know God, and he know her heart...
Could he somehow commute my sentence,
I've already been tried and convicted,
sentenced and socially evicted, persecuted and crucified.
Emotionally I've died then revived and convicted
circumcised before spiritually being baptized,
cried the waters from my eyes,
I'm physically payin' my tithes and,
read about 28 calendars in my spare time
I'm tired of being tied to sudden change and infliction,
the pain this game inflictin' is far more fruitful
then the change we claim as
our love ones this fiasco actually bangs and maims.
Who really be the victims?

you can't just pick them out of line-ups and
depict them as mindless, call us spineless- yet -
compell us to compromise our sanity,
in vain inside a cage where we rage in profanity.
Man it be insane how they keep bangin'
our brains out our cranium.
Titanium hearts,
abusing us hard, for
recreation,
regardless of any consideration to what type of shape we in.
God created them men,
but the system created them spiritless Homosapiens where they
keep rapin' them with restrictions. That's just more convictions
I'm tired of being tied to these worldly addictions
like commissary, mail and visiting hours or
looking over at the watchtower where the watcher in the tower
towers over me makin' me drop my head,
cuzz the lead in his riffle is power, ready to shower me.
Don't get me wrong I ain't no coward, not me, see,
but I ain't no fool either
and I damn sure ain't gone let them devour me like food
                                              either.
It's hard to believe it, but, he's a man like me and
we both are burnin' in the ether.
We'll probably be sand before we realize that
I ain't just no ordinary man neither,
man we men not fetus
so believe this when I speak this or forever remain speechless
while this speech is speakin' to silence yo' speaker
cuzz I'm speakin' to you!

Cure for Cancer

Don't really care to talk about it
cause my cure is my cure and
not one other could remedy me an antidote
seeing as though my only medicine is the mental of a woman
who is into my venues and veracious visions and views
her very sight in my don't and do's
are harmoniously fused synchronized in such a way where
we work as a machine meticulously crafted to conquer
what comes dare I do say the diabolical diagnosis
is one terminal because it trains
the thirst never switches track in tack and attack my
neuro transmitters emitting energy undetectable by M.R.I.s
x-rays and toxicology reports
her presence contorts my spinal column and cortex
causing convulsions from which I cringe
insert the I.V.
when she walks by me cause I'm just that weak for her
without a spasm or a coma I feel her
in my bones like radiation from chemo
I wish she would just let me go
and find her another host to infest with her rapid delusion
soul smothering swift spreading fungus of promise
damn the difibulators!
of another will come later
I'm fine with flat line
I don't care to see you later
I'm walking in to the light
don't whisper prayers
the surgeon save me, nor beg me to fight
this my death bed
put me on the cold slab
tag my toe
this my answer and
cure for cancer.

AFTERMATH

I am the effect of what poverty caused!

The direct descendent of lowered expectation but the physical manifestation of resolve.

Motivation by the mitigating factors that weren't factored in when defeatist mentalities counted me out.

Now I stand stout,

erect even, driven by the timeless energy emitted by the internal universe that I control.

The calamity that challenged me challenged Haiti and as did the ancestral bloodline of a liberated people, I overcame my catastrophe by diligently dissecting sections of broken dreams while, extracting extensions of perseverance from the brothers and sisters eternally exuding due diligence, then I externalized the overdue fortitude of founding fathers responsible for the contusions of a bruised nation.

I vehemently express my discontent with the absentee me. Announcing my resentment through my scowl, the wrinkling of my brow displays the disdain for ignored prophecy clairvoyantly prophesied by me.

Caged intellect can't cage intellect.

I project outwardly with tenacity.

How dare they imprison me and expect me to come out the same way I went in

When I showed up I went in.

Perpetuating one stereotype while eradicating another.

Freedom's my mother, Mandela my daddy, I Malcolm X the dictionary daily.

Idiosyncratically Succinct!

So don't ask me if I'm ready for the world, you're better off asking the world if it's ready for me!

Aftermath, what comes after the storm?!?

Ask Katrina whose still bleeding five years after her beating, or better yet, survey the surviving love ones left to cope with the 911 tragedy.

Not the aristocrats who transformed reform when foreigners flew planes into the towers, or those cowards who decided to stand by and watch while an entire city was drowning.

I'll do you one better, solicit the parents of the murdered school children bewildered by the echoing cries in the distance.

The need to reach out to an arm that won't reach back, the longing for a hug or the romance of a kiss.

Now riddle me this, would you even exist if bureaucratic antics wouldn't label this as simple semantics and use the necessary language to bring leverage to the destruction brought forth by ignored pleas.

It was the ignored pleas of equality that created the atrocities we witness.

Not just in the distance but up close.

The wars has hatched domestic terrorist who lay eggs at our back door and the hypocrisy that is the freedom of religion was depleted when we began to equate terror with every Quran bearer.

Terrorist are nefarious no matter what religion or hue. Let's not forget that Christian Crusaders were terrorist too,

for every cause there's an effect.

Imprison untapped potential, I'll return educated with the education to educate.

Drown me in the waters of New Orleans, I'll resurrect the 5th ward with mental jewels to rebuild stronger.

Under fund my schools and mis-educate my sons and daughters I'll home school scholars on your dollar with the sole purpose to take your power.

Elect Bush for two terms then allow him to exhaust the inherited surplus to pay his staff.

Obama, will be the
Aftermath.

LET ME BE THERE FOR YOU

Listen, Queen I'm forced to deal with myself and live my mistakes every day.
It's understood you've been scared by others and the games they play.
How could they even bear to hurt you and watch the tears crawl down your lovely face!
I promise to never do you wrong, but be that hero to chase the pain away.

Let me start by apologizing for all those that chose to do you wrong.
Including myself for allowing my situation to take me so far away from home.
It just hurts me Ma, to know that I've left you so all alone.
But I want you to remember what we have, we must keep holding on.

My word is bond, you don't have to worry about me ever abusing your trust.
I've too many years already making plans and thinking about us.
I can't lie though, at least ten percent of that was all about lust.
Meaning that the total one hundred percent says a fifty/fifty love is a must.

I was born to be your only man and there's nothing to replace that.
If I could reverse the hands of time I would follow a different track.
I've never lost you Ma, but every day I want you back.
I love to love you baby, now how much love is that.

Your love is an illness, but I like the effects on my brain.
It's like you shot me up and now permanently in my veins.
Look at the years that have passed us bye and ain't nothing changed.
I pray to stay happily ever after and bless you with my last name.

This is a guaranty through sickness and health for better or worst.
Trust me I do love you and priceless is what you're worth.
Know that I am going to do everything in my power to make this work.
I only want to see you smile baby even if it's just your sexy smirk.

From the very first moment I saw you; I remember the look in your eyes.
You have always been so confident, but when you spoke you were shy.
Queen you were so beautiful that it was intimidating I can't lie.
You are my only one and from you my emotions I want hide.

Just to have you whisper in my ear got me hooked for a lifetime.
Truly I do adore also appreciate your choice being the same as mine.
Please don't show no worries Ma, because every little things going to be fine.
For you only my life is an open book with no need to read between the lines.

I've said it before, heaven is what we make of it and hell is what we go through.
Everything that I have belongs to my queen too.
I belong in your corner for whatever you choose to do.
All you need is to open your heart and let me be there for you.

CRUSHED GRAPES

Disgruntled definitions of what's depicted as being a, REAL MAN can
sometimes
be deceptive if the description grunted is coming from a feminine
perception,
Wait a minute before you go on the defensive!!!
My offensive position in this petition is not meant to offend you, but
rather wed
our indifferences by eloping across the threshold of gender to genuinely
cross the
lines between, Love & Hate.
And I hate to be the bearer of bad news before your wedding date, but to
date, it
seems like she who jumps the broom too soon, dreams get swept away.
Crushed Grapes leaves a bad taste, but still you drink from this cup when
you
choose a groom who lacks the mental bristles detrimental to sweeping
you off
your feet mentally.
And since you've been bewitched mentally, your commitment forces you
to ride
this broomstick infinitely.
I feel you when you say, "What does it take to find a REAL MAN,
mentally?"
Well, history tells us ancient poets scripted scrolls that interpret the
intimacy of
Patience, so let us pay attention to its virtue as it pours its verses in out of
vessels
vacancies.
See, I'm not an atheist, but when it comes to the religious faithful of
fables on face
book who paste quotes as favorites, I BECOME PAGAN, but still I
strain my ear
and listen to these iffy inflammation of information as if it could save me,
to raise me from my grave way of thinking, you must first drink from my
cup, but
the lady who drinks too much, will be the one who betrays me,

the daughter of perdition who takes her men, shaking not stirred, which
leaves
most women's mental martini's with olives that sinks to the bottom, the
olive is
indicative to the hearts omnipotence, but it's obvious that the vodka &
tonic
elevates your tolerance to tolerate the imbalance of men that inhabits
your safe
place.
I can pitty that, but I'd rather give you the bareback of wisdom that you
might
piggy back to understanding, willingly. But you compare me to wine
vicariously,
as if the roots of my vines have never been found in the valley.
and although I hate to battle the earth that gave birth to my grapevine, I
must
crush your grapes because of what I heard you say through the grapevine,
See, hypocrisy is the wine of violence, so let's have a moment of silence
while I
silence the hypocrites who stumble and stagger over Internet flattery.
Sadly, your life has been flat-lined by flat wine for far too long, so I'll be
expedient about giving you the organic ingredients needed to complete
you.
See, grapes that makes a great wine is plentiful, so how is it that in a time
of
plenty your vats keep coming up empty?
Maybe it's because your views are tilted, which spills the juices instilled in
your
mental distillery, a REAL MAN is vintage, so the pickings are reserved
for the
well deserved who served as a wine dresser when he was still an untilled
vineyard.
Just because there's a sparkle in your eyes for sparkling wine doesn't
mean that
you're deserving, certainly sore eyes can leave you thirsty...
...so not to disrespect you, I will pleasure you by poetically wiping the
tears from
your eyes changing your waters into wine,

no more crying!
I'm that bottle of wine you've been whining over, and although I'm not Barttles &
James, I'm a man with emotions that are bottled up,
but you can't seem to muster up the strength to un-cork my sustenance, which
screws you, because the corkscrew you used to get to my booze, couldn't get through,
and even if you get me to open up, you know not what to toast to. But if we can
touch hearts and salute to a solution suitable enough for us to drink to, only then
will I salute you...
...who are you to compare me to wine? You can't mix me with drinks, my vine
doesn't swing that way, but for the sake of mingling we can mingle, but just don't
crush my grapes.
See, it takes ages of fermentation to formulate a form of man with flavor, but it's
the impatient taste testers that experience the bitter sweet taste of a tasteless man,
Intoxicating, ain't it?
You drank the wine of violence in excess, and now you're calling Earl, but my
name is Robert, but I'll phone Tyrone's home in hopes that he'll hand over a
potent dosage of poetry for those who are hung-over.
See, I'm a man hands down even when you throw your hands up, it's not what
you throw up that defines me, I know that your regurgitation is induced by the
frustration of you not being able to find me.
Yeah, I'm a REAL MAN, and in my stance I stand as a beacon of hope who throw
ropes to emotional wine-heads whose boats docked because they weren't anchored in love, MAN OVERBOARD!!
Isn't a man at all, real men may wobble, but they don't fall down, instead

they toe
the line by towing the line that entwines hearts and minds spiritually,
but you seek me sparingly, and rather beseech French benefits by sipping
lavishly.
A REAL MAN can't be set as a standard concerning name brands, it is
these same
name brands that end up being lame, all because his name was ringing,
but tell me, where's your ring at?
Is it safe to say that you laid with Allyze, and let Crystal have his way?
Now tell
me, who picked up the check? You even had sex with Moet and wasn't
satisfied,
Was it his bottle top that popped too soon, and left you wet?
Again, a REAL MAN is more than just a brand name, it is the quality of
wine in
his wineskin that determines the quality of man within,
See, I use to be a Mad Dog when I was 20/20 years ago, until that special
someone came and twist my cap, in fact, she found me wrapped in a
brown paper
bag doing bad, but took a chance on me.
Then she poured me emotionally into her physical cup, now spiritually
and
mentally her cup runneth over,
I'm that thug that caused her joy to bubble up, and when it comes to
Love...
...we **Crush Grapes** and say, bottoms up...

A SPECTACULAR SPEECH

A spectacular speech speaking on the struggles
in our streets won't suffice to stop the slaughter
of our seeds.
Should I continue speaking slow speed? something like
suspense before the stainless steel squeeze
six shots in small shorty--
small shoe size. Leaving small shorty on a stretcher
surrounded by surgical staff. Senseless strife.
I sense shorty spirit in the sky.
Now suddenly society sympathize with seconds of silence.....
Stop and smell the stench
sorta like stanky smoke from a square.
Scriptures and surgs--
sighted souls want to share spiritual secrets
So what's the secrets to staying safe when
stuck in a situation so serious like sedation?
A small sister was getting rapped since subordination
to her stepfather. His sexual stimulation.
Somebody do something. Sanction Satan
or show a sign.
Why the sun slow to shine on something so sublime and sensitive?
I shed streams.
The slave master said scream
as he took his switch and slapped his slave with sixty swings.
Imagine snap shots of the scene.
Blood seemed to spew and spout.
The slave was sixteen. He suffered without a shout.
So strong and stout. Surviving down south.
The slavery system stole somebody's spouse.
The Willie Lynch syndrome separated the Black House
like splitting a Siamese.
I still see signs in society. The status quo--
no signs of sobriety.
They snorting and sniffing that snow.
Sin sickens the soul.
State Street slick on the slow.

Sister swift on the stroll.
Sucker select. Stupid for sure.
Syphilis specks soliciting sex so she can spend solely on
smoking a suicidal substance, and now she's skinny.
At first she was slugging, but she wasn't a slut then.
Some sleaze bag snuck in and
got her strutting in short skirt and
looking so sad. So I say to my sister and
to my people--
Assalamu 'alaikum!

They say we don't, they hope we ain't
they say we won't, they hope we can't
conquer the crippling critical cancer
that corrupts courtships causing a
crumbling called communicational cracks

they hope we can't, they say we won't
they say we don't, they hope we ain't
built to last the laps of the taunting
torturous toxic tyrant called time

they hope we can't, they say we won't
they hope we can't, they say we don't
stand a chance to claim the
coveted celestial climatic closeness
that is felt by two souls becoming one

they hope we can't, they say we don't
they hope we ain't, they say we won't
ever be the beautiful Mr. & Miss
with the fabulous family envied by
societies upper echelon as the one's
that made it through hell's storm and
beyond

they don't, they ain't, they won't
and they can't ever understand
the love in our band
of woman & man.

The End

It's the participation and preparation for the anticipation that feeds the
hunger of the
devastation this world is awaiting come 2012, leaving our planet in peril.

I've envisioned human beings walking the streets without hope when
meteorologists
release reports of unimaginable events.

Offspring's of tsunamis breed with earthquakes demolishing buildings
and states from
coast to coast.

Fear stricken people pleading to make amends before this Age end.
When will it all end?

Will it be our Sins that will produce those stout winds or the so call sins
of our ancestors
causing the Earth's axis to shift swiftly, disarranging the compass we
once knew?

A world wide talk-athon performs live on center stage, in concerts
discussing topics
concerning the division of the roads.

I suppose this date derived from those of the Mayans because with their
minds they
decided there's no further reason to continue time. And the Chiefs of our
days
compliment their prophecy.

Tell me people that you're reading between the lines and you're not
blind!

Game time, covertly chanted among the union while planning to move
us around like

sacrificial pawns on the board, divide & conquer at its best (Haves and
Have-nots.)

The new millennium was a dreaded lost, it's the sound bites that
masticate and spit out
our independent thoughts leaving the mind mesmerized searching
through the rubbish
aimlessly.

So don't be beguiled, they're just being loud, we have the power to
change the plans of
those who covet to be the top shareholder of the land.

TEACH ME...

I must admit, I'm oblivious to the wonders of your mind. The cerebral chambers of celestial transcendence that separates you from the failed lessons of the past.

I've learned from those lessons what not to do and from my studies I've acquired an intense desire to master the biography that verifies your verity.

The severity of my speech releases an unseen focus that explains the complexities accompanied by guileless devotion.

As trivial as you have appeared in the eyes of others, my attention is substantially attentive to the needs of the unsettled. Your willingness to compromise has compromised the judiciousness that categorizes me as a fable, but truth be witnessed, I can provide the honor reserved solely to honor you…if you allow me to and if my demonstration of affection doesn't please you, I offer my attention while giving you the uninterrupted permission to...

...Teach me how to love you!

What's understood need not be explained but, misunderstanding of the explained confuses the understood.

If I am to figure out your mental and emotional entanglement on my own, who's to say, my rights won't be your wrongs?

I'll be better suited with tutelage, leaving nothing to be refuted and if you tell me what's right for you is right for two, I won't dispute it.

Baby I'm your student. Eagerly engrossed in every tool used to help me excel and you exhale.

You don't need hooked on phonics to reach me, I'm hooked on you. Addicted to the secrets that secure the vulnerabilities exploited by the masculine masquerades that occupied your days before I came.

Those fools who fooled you have been replaced. The proof of accuracy is in your face and though these are simply words on a page, I'm speaking directly to you.

The constructor that offers this pledge extends his hand along with the sublime physical principle designated exclusively to service the satisfaction desired on every level.

I'm here to subdue the uneasiness produced by pretenders who profited from your despair.

The refulgence of your smile is all I ask in return and since the passion deserving of you is long overdue, I surrender myself and ask that you,

Teach me how to love you!

Teach me how to touch those sensual spots ignored by the selfishness, educate me through the swivel of your hips if I should lick or suck, or go deeper and harder or maybe slow down and coast you to climax.

Indoctrinate me with your pleasure principals. When you want to ride it or get it from the side or lay flat on your stomach as I kiss the back of your neck and gently pull your hair.

Instruct me with a detailed example on how gentle you want your clitoris touched. Message your breast as I watch, then kiss my lips with extra enthusiasm as your orgasm articulates the arc in your back and the tightness in your waist.

Train me on spontaneity with an afternoon quicky in the rain or, maybe an elevator showcase of sexual candor at your workplace.

We can even tease the tourist with a touch of oral copulation promoting public displays of affection as we exhibit how great of a student I am and teacher you are.

And if by chance I fail this class, I'll re—enroll in your course until I'm declared a scholar in the art of loving you.

So, make me your pupil! Make me your exhaustive indulgence, your craving of desire.

Make me your expugnable infatuation, your infallible fidelity and I'll promise to stay true.

I'm here willing and able when you're ready to,

Teach me how to love you.

HEY MA...

Hey Ma

Just sitting here thinking, and Ma I find myself so amazed.
Who would've guessed that you'll still be by my side after years and
countless days?
I can't lie, I'm guilty of not believing your promise of not going
anywhere. You've earned everything that's mine to give and my word is
I'll be there.

Hey Ma
Do know you are more than any world to me and this in truth I mean!
You are a vision of beauty a true goddess and my earth is much more
than a queen.
Many of men may witness your beauty. But I've got your heart, body, and
mind.
Many of women have tried to stand in your place but it's only a perfect
fit for you inside.

Hey Ma
Find it selfish of me, but I'm glad other men have missed what I see in
you.
That's why I'm ready, willing, and able to give you all the credit I feel is
past due.
In each and every aspect for sure I'm proud to be your one and only
man.
Here's a toast to us ma, because you are mine and more than a woman.

Hey Ma
The very first moment I saw you I couldn't help but to stare.
That perfect moment is when I knew all of my love was meant for you to
share.
The most beautiful thing a celestial being that only Godly eyes should
see.
Like Etta James, I'd rather go blind than to see you walk away from me.

Hey Ma

Every time I close my eyes I go way back down memory lane.
Today I stumbled upon your photograph and to this day your beauty still remains.
There goes my baby and she's always looking better than ever.
Chivalry ain't dead for you I'll lay my coat over a puddle and in rain cover your head
from the weather.

Hey Ma
This one here is to show every little bit of my appreciation.
I thank you for everything you bring to the table you're my greatest inspiration.
That inspires and keeps on holding me up just by holding me down.
In adversity you always keep me planted on solid ground.

Hey Ma
You are the reason that our love knows no limit.
The times we spend together do believe that I cherish every minute.
We are already there whenever it comes to withstanding the test of time.
Move me no mountain to be with you the highest one I would climb.

Hey Ma
Love is love and for sure love is what you are.
You are my universe and I am your sun the brightest star.
As we lay, may we dream to the imagination of our most wonderful dreams!
So that when we awake we can bring those dreams to exist as real things.

Hey Ma
Don't you ever think for a minute that I'll ever walk away or let you go!
There are many women in the world, but it's only you I want to know.
Never hold your head down I love your shine so continue to smile.
Even if I'm not there in the physical continue to think of me and I'll be around.

Hey Ma
I thought that I should remind you that you're always on my mind.

This piece is poetry in motion and only you were thought about in every line.
So may these words help to make light of your day.
At the very least always shine for me Ma and keep a smile on your face.

FROZEN SUN

My heart is huge like a fiery love
trapped within an icy force field above.
Yep, it is something like a frozen
Sun up in the sky before the world begun.
Not like a lit match inside an ice cube-
my heart is huge.
And it shines no longer during the day,
which now makes my flowers long for my ray.
If I could defrost what is in my chest
behind the ozone layer of ribs and flesh,
I would, but what I need now is just you-
my heart is huge.

Sonnet

Environmental Genocide

Sitting in wonderment
captured by the thought of you,
struggling to hold on to a dream
that never was;
Only my misplaced hope of preparation
slowly coming to the reality,
of my mental masturbation...
I thought you were real.
Giving you everything I had of me-
giving up numerous opportunities,
I was blinded by your allure...
Taking all my steps without thought
thinking your love was for sure.
Admittingly not all was in vain,
you taught me that your love
and my ignorance-
is truly one in the same...
No one's fault but my own.
I gave my unconditional love,
for you I'd get down or lay down;
The ultimate sacrifice!
I was willing to put it all on the line.
Separation and time pointed out to me
that I was fussin' and fightin'-
for something that was never even mine.
I intimately knew every curb of you,
familiarized like the creases on my palm.
Tired and sad, and lonely you are-
Still singin' the same old song.
It's been ten years now without your scent,
though, I can't knock what you do.
The difference is that you've gotten worse-
Constantly viewing your claim to fame
continuously taking my brothaz and sistaz
for a ride...
In that long black hearse.

Never known to be a man of religion
but now all I can do is pray.
Hoping to be living example for many,
denying you the opportunity to take my
loved-ones away.
Maybe I'm just a man time has made bitter,
simply because you lied.
Yet I still can't deny the fact that
you're my environmental genocide.

The creation of she who was the creation of me

Life stands lonely in the light of its existence.
Searching itself for the fulfillment of love lost and pastense.
   Vividly- the sight of its pain is blinding, and while feeling endlessly and no finding of satisfaction, there begins contraction in motion with retraction and formed is its heart.
   Physically designed to play the part of providing sense within its self while becoming dense and casting a shadow of she, the existence of light captured in life's longing to be and hence forth its longing for love was given for all to see!

   The woman, black woman who out of darkness stood like a diamond amongst running waters of the Nile, Heaven in her smile, infinity in her eyes, support in her thighs and healing in every tear she cries.
   In her stance she held an embraced life like nothing else could, pumping her love through its every vein and artery until man stood, escaping the lonely eons of coldness by his light being redirected and reflected throughout space from her face....the embodiment of God's grace!

   Cut and chiseled to perfection, she gave a second birth to beauty's projection, ordering what was once empty and hopeless into crystals of jade and sapphire, setting the element of oxygen a fire when running through infant lungs.
   And I screamed! as she pushed me out of her matrix into arms, kissing my lips with her charm, so deeply that I became entranced in past visions of me sleeping under her heart beat,
   Rhythms of my pain emerged from her heart as she chanted peace my King, Peace! My pain became my heart, my heart my life, my life my wife, and my wife was no other than my plight...which was to love

I SEE DEAD PEOPLE!

I See Dead People! Walking & breathing like, leaches feeding off internal bleeding, with suction cups attached to the influx of pity parties.

I went to pity parties early where they served shots of cyanide laced with Red Bulls filled with anthrax.

It was there at those parties that I joined a conglomerate berated by the over exaggerated.

Less means more, meaning, the less you appreciate self, the more I'm enriched by the diminishment of your self wealth.

I See Dead People..., night stalkers in need of light to see themselves. Not the internal light magnified by that internal right to define self.

I'm speaking of the external light that's guided & dictated by moving objects & obstructive structures used to conceal the high beams of self-esteem.

I See Dead People…crowned with the glory from frivolous stories, told by fictitious authority that mummifies the torsos of mental embryos that loses life with every Prada bag or Gucci shoe accessorized with a Louis Vutton jump suit.

Resuscitated by the envious looks & revived by the adoring eyes of someone else, but strangled by the reflective view reflecting you in the nude, hanged by the absence of someone else's brand name attached to the garments connected to your brand name & when I close my eyes in an attempt to escape this scene, my dream become the sequel, because even then, I see the suicidal corpus of, Dead People.

Blown out of proportion

I can stare out into the ether
to the elements transmute
and loot the essence,
polute every plane
to alter the inaudible vibrations
that refrains my brain from containing' lessons.
Feel like I'm psychologically chained
to violations involving vicious cycles
of violence that's pitted against my love
and its demise is despised like disobedient disciples.
They pound the pavement in search of
economical enterprises that rise and fall
like urban pharmaceuticals that's unsuitable for ya'll.
I'm in the jaws of death, grinded to dust then
blew between prison walls for all to see underneath
the universal laws I'm unique in my flaws as we speak,
and the difference between me and a lot of people
is I'm seeing the truth
though my situation's bleak.
It reeks with decomposed aspects of my soul
the cold components that comprise my existence
on this globe.
I stroll perpendicular to particular vision of life,
the light.
I breathe light from the tight confines of deprived space
and time combined with ill minds who's angles ain't right.
Got the audacity to consider us dark Angel's at night.
My ancestors were a lucrative franchise
I'm speaking commodity wise
badgered but never broken while being dehumanized
and birthed those society coin disenfranchised.
Their lies are political asylum, silence them
with violence, divide them for centuries to provide them
with penitentiaries, strip its prisoners from poverty;
A plantation hybrid, obviously. It's modernized
robbery minus the 2-11 code.

Script us with legal logistics
can't compete with law universities bold linguistics.
The story is always told after the soul is sold
money is the root of all evil...7 fold
so let it unfold.
I swear the endz'll lead you to the beginning of the road,
and that was his first offense.
I'm convinced- them the same people that lynched Michael Vick-
It's sick how they twist my grey's anatomy out of proportion,
like Isaiah Washington's character dramatically,
graphmactically
emasculating masculinity to publically castrate
any black figure to destroy our identity
and here we are kicking each other's ass in the media
like we our own enemy.
Now I can see how things get blown out of proportion.
Media stay f--king people for personal purposes...
ain't that extortion?
society got me feeling like a misrepresentation
or a miscarriage of conscious...A late term abortion.

Street

My cipher so hard I crack concrete
I feel every bump and pothole, I can't catch a green light
Drugs in my life like I got full healthcare coverage
Signs in the ether say the fast lane is a one way road
My main drag is a known hoe stroll where girls make you u-turn
The avenue is a expressway to hell, no pay toll
No construction just decay, hood full of garbage men
I've seen many kids go down the wrong route and life meet ahead
Come to the crossroads and the wrong turn can make you one of the lost
boys.
The block like dirt, you can't keep your hands clean
They call me the budget of revenue, pay homage and get your meal ticket
If lips seal shut like asphalt, suckers will stay free of my execution
I'm restitution for the lawless who feel life owe them a refund
Rendezvous where the dead found live
Where I've seen many place their feet on the path of Dr. King
And lose their drive, or lose their lives
Pain blood clot drain, after being washed
Twice in one day, strays, slaying victims is the only way to stay clean
Screams echo loudly but go unheard down the spine of my
Back blocks and alleys
I took the souls of black boys in the heat of the night, and made
Their favorite logo a sign on a live wire
I am the boardwalk of recession, I take your life possessions
And your life essence, and leave your corpse on a tombstone sidewalk
I am a grave, I'm just that deep
I am the streets!

This was supposed to be poetry

This was supposed to be poetry
& so be it if it's suppose to be,
but if spoken right, this spoken word
should sum up into one smoldering verb.
Hate, & I know it's atrocious
but I'ma lost cause, hopeless, hateful
so I embrace my trade, I'm even proud of my label.
But hey, what choice do you leave me
when hate is my hobby & you make it so easy.
You sell drugs to the people I love
but I suppose our poverty justifies your thug.
You shoot my hood up & make my children victims
& all the while you tell me to quit snitchin'. But I reject that,
& if that's your "gansta" then how could I ever respect that?
Accept that? NEVER, why would I?
sit idly by & say nothing, how could I?
Should I be afraid of being labeled a hater
& let you take my voice like a disabled debater?
Nah, I don't think so,
I think it better of me to step up & better us
but if you got a better idea then batter up.
I'm riding wit it if we riding for right, saddle up.
I've had enough already, you proved you tough already
I get it, you hardcore & I'm a chump already.
Whatever, I just wanna be better than what we've been
cause it ain't been adding up no matter what the numbers been.
I hate seein' you being fly
when you ain't got rent money & you don't know why.
Am I a hater cuz I hate you for standing for hate?
If so, I'm the poster child for the standard of hate,
& I'm fine wit, being defined & entwined with it,
but how can it be hate if love is aligned wit it?
Good question right?
But hey, what do I know, I'm just a hater
or maybe I just think it's about time for you to wake up.

A Conscious Thought

What's So - - - Damned Funny?

Something has been perplexing me,
And I was wondering if somebody, anybody,
Can supply me an answer to this very simple question,
All I want to know is...
<u>What's So - - - Damned Funny?</u>

"Laugh Now Cry Later", is what the wise one's breathed on me.
Why is it that so many of us still don't understand?
So many of us are blind,
But only think we can see.
<u>"The same thing that makes you laugh will also make you cry"</u>
We've heard this phrase our entire lives.
But how many of us stop and pause,
Contemplate and meditate,
And really wrap our minds around what this means?
I hear sounds of laughter,
And see smiling faces all around me,
But I still don't understand...
<u>What's So - - - Damned Funny?</u>

Because I also hear the lies of war mongering politicians,
And I see the consequences of their racist policies.
I see the hungry and the homeless,
The unemployed and the poor.
Marijuana, crack cocaine, crystal meth and ecstasy
Is ravishing another generation of our young ones.
Two out of every ten African-American men
Are either in jail, prison, on parole or probation.
And why do we get more time for the same crimes?
We spend more years in prison than we do in high school or college.
We have children that we can't even support.
We are being stereotyped, profiled, programmed and conditioned for
failure.
Yet I see too many of us walking around supporting silly grins and
smiles,
laughing out loud.

But I just don't get the punch line...
What's So - - - Damned Funny?

We have increasing numbers of black men
Creeping around on the 'down-low'
And our black women are caught up in the fad of having girlfriends.
H.I.V. AND A.I.D.S. is real!
This virus is alive and well
And flourishing in the bodies of those who took "IT" for a joke.
"Laugh Now, Cry Later"!, Live carefree, careless, and reckless now, but
sooner
or later, you will pay the consequences.
This is the lessons the years have taught me.
There has been too much laughter,
Too much blood has been shed,
Too much sweat,
And too many tears.
Who else has had more obstacles to overcome,
More stumbling blocks in our path,
More trials and tribulations?
They say, "If it doesn't kill you, it'll make you stronger".
Well if that's true,
Who else is stronger than us!
Who else had to survive what we as a people have had to endure?
Our history has been nothing to laugh at.
We were stolen from our homeland,
Sold as slaves,
Forced into labor for hundreds of years; beating, lynching, racism,
segregation,
oppression, discrimination, jails, institutions and death, and police
brutality.
This is our legacy of our treatment in America and it is our burden.
I wonder...
Do my people smile, tell jokes and signify
Because the reality of our situation is just too painful to acknowledge?
I don't know...
Maybe it's just me; because to think we as a people have too many
problems

and issues to be wasting time, energy and mind power by thinking up
funny
things to say to make each other laugh.
Let's stop being silly, and let's get serious, because if you ask me...
<u>Ain't A Damned Thing Funny!!</u>

Written By
E. M. Hicks Jr. A.K.A. Abdullah Ilyas El-Mahdi Hassan

Chapter two

Alone At Night

In this corner wearing his heart on his sleeve
we have weighing 210. 5' 7' the number 1 contender
fighting out of pure heart and faith   "Forever Hopeful"
And in this corner we have the champion, ticker kicker,
suicide causer, midnight hour heartache insomia---"Pseudo Love"

Ding! round number 1

Hopeful come out swinging his powerful pen & paper stroke
but Pseudo Love counters with a promise to write more jab
staggering Hopeful but Hopeful shakes it off
and is back pedaling on old letters
sniffing the remnants of perfume-
Hopeful throws a combination of epic proportions
Love you card hook, six page love letter left, and the
infamous three-way phone call uppercut
putting Pseudo Love up against the ropes
and we might have a new champ tonight----wait!
what's this-
Pseudo Love side steps Hopeful
pressing 1 telling Hopeful to call back later
cuz Pseudo Love is about to leave for work
throwing a tripple body shot with a man's voice
saying, "whose on the phone baby" putting Hopeful in rage
opening him up for a flush chin shot-
Hopeful drops his guard saying, "who's that you're talking to
in the background-"
the silent but deadly no voice staggers Hopeful----
the phone hangs up
setting Pseudo love up for the big finish-
Hopeful is saved by the bell
of announcer, Can't let go
now back for another round of trouble.

Ding! round 2

Hopeful comes out looking good bobbing and weaving around
Pseudo Love with his looking at old photo skills
throwing a beautiful jab of flash back
to the sexy jeans he bought his Queen
on their anniversary sending Pseudo Love
to his knees, regaining his composure Pseudo Love springs up
with crushing blows of infrequent mail
false promises of visits combo
the oh I forgot your birthday cross
stumbling Hopeful looks dazed
as Pseudo Love comes raining down the fatal lights out
chin checker dear John letter....

1 She don't love you
2 You're a sucker
3 You lied to yourself
4 Don't trust again
5 She don't care
6 She ripped out your heart
7 Stop listening
8 Don't ever bear your soul
9 Know when to walk away
10 She broke bad a long time ago

YOUR OUT....................!

and still champion, Pseudo Love
Hopeful says he wants a rematch...
...see you next time people on internal conflict
I'm your host, Alone At Night.

THE FIRST TIME

Poof my sanity.

No humanity.
Just her.

       A bright place.

Did heaven fall?
the sight of her face.

       Goddess status.
       Nude.

Making me worship her
fattest curve.

       Fantasy ass.

Fantasies holdfast.
       No magazines.

This is mine.

       My luscious queen.

Woman in my mind,
       of my dream—
       so fine.

So divine.

       A dime piece
in three piece lingerie

       Incense blowing.
       Melody flowing,

and just knowing
this is real.

      Passionate kissing.
      Lingering feels.

She moans,
      then squeals
as my tongue roams,
      her core buzz.

Foreplay my love.

      Juices flood.

Jubilation.

Anticipation.

      Less patient.

      Where is it?

Enter the warmth.

      Exquisite.

      Her grip so wet.

Never forget
the first time.
my first climb
      to climax.

Wolf Pack

My heart a frozen tundra
lyrics is religion, my poems thunder
I spit hunger
fall on winter with axe picks
then sleep for the summer.
Spring through the Philippines like a monsoon
disappear then reappear a tornado in Maine
I ain't a storm,
I'm a season of hurricanes!
crusade like Christians in chains
I ain't dissing just insisting on change
persistent and strange
my visions deranged
conditioned for pain
my wolf pack
apostles with the world on our backs.
We growl then attack.
Canines in the mist of sheep
scatter the heard then feast.
Alpha male I'm a beast.
Obese from politics and conceit
go to sleep in the clutches of deceit
no surrender no defeat
bow before my feet
I got fangs for teeth.
My inspiration comes from above
it's raining words
spitting flames and verbs
the pains absurd
but I will not be deterred!
go to war like Bosnians and Serbs
my bullets is mental-
ricochet then curve
f*ck grafitti, I scribble hieroglyphs on the curb.

Chrissha

She came within the grey mist of the rain,
her eyes were impregnated with misfortune.
She was the first born daughter of a war—torn love
buried her mother in the red dirt of her homeland.
She sang a psalm in her native tongue,
talked with the moon as she danced like her ancestors.
There's a beauty in her roasted Somalian clay complexion,
I watched the Sun's reflection as it laid lazily
on her shoulder blade.
She said she swam to America...I laughed,
she showed me the shackled marks around her feet and neck.
I don't mean to sound shallow but her middle passage
was deeper than the Atlantic,
she was destined for cotton fields and restless nights
where she was raped and plundered.
No wonder she pushed out a healthy man—child
with blood in his eyes,
so despised he was sold for a three legged mule the same night.
It was so quiet you could hear the Angels in heaven crying.
She said she hadn't slept since the Messiah died.
I was standing there dying inside,
So I asked her why sell your body then?
She said it pays more than dancing in videos,
besides she said she love the hours, she could walk for hours,
I tied her shoe laces,
commence walking through her past life,
it took us 4 hours to get through her last year of pain
and I can finally see how her dreams were murdered.
I even saw her get murdered,
I mean sitting in an abortion clinic had to hurt her.
But she come out looking amazing,
it must have been the xtacy pills that had her dancing
the Flamingo.
Said she was in Spain, could have been Casablanca in Morrocco.
Her Moorish dress got torn in the fiasco.
She sobbed in arabic,

then told me not to mention it
because she hated to cover her face up.
Such a lovely face to deface,
so I turned my back on her and walked away.
She was an abusive spouse,
and this love-jones was killing me.
I'm gone Chrissha!!!

CRY BABY

I cry lamentations because of life's revelations.
I hope you can interpret a broken souls language because,
a cold soul knows no RosettaStone.
I spit spoken words to dry bones with words well-spoken
in hopes to add muscle to ligament but,
what does it profit men if I was to lament tears lyrically?
Jesus wept bitterly after John cried in the wilderness,
now tell me, should I cry like they did or,
should I cry like Jonah and wail from the belly?
This is my last will and testament, I won't see next year,
because kids killing kids plagued me with high blood pressure.
I'm just hyperthetically speaking like erroneous teachings.
This is my symmetry speaking and, I'm 6ft width no inches,
and you wonder why my thoughts are so deep and reek like cemeteries.
I watched a boy get slained on the news earlier and
I tried to feel his pain but, "Breaking News" came saying,
"Sara Palin is touring Des' Moines during her political campaign:
I wanna blame BET and the rap game for placating a felonious
movement,
but that'll be a stereotype like, Sony.
Another shorty got murked around 5:00 in the morning and,
he was just feeling horny like any other adolescent,
until that masked robber brought him that "T-Pain,"
and brung him dread like the head of "Lil Wayne."
Dueces! they "Chris Brown'ed" another youth and
it was sensless because he got killed for "Young Money,"
some say it was just "50 cent."
This is why my thoughts are fugitives, I'm lost
like the "Fugees!" lost "Laurynn Hill."
Somebody summons the "Roots"
because the death rate in our communities is, "Badu,"
I mean, "Common,"
forgive me my words "Twista,"
and I slurr like a "Lunatic" from St. Louis,
or like that lil sista found twisted behind her school in E. St. Louis.
I cried for that baby but,

does that make me a cry baby?
I cried til my "left Eye" was "Puffy." but
just two tears in the bucket compared to her mother.
I have nothing left,
it's like my tears can't propel themselves, so they ebb
back to that place and start over again.
They say a man aint suppose to cry,
so I place my tears in a bottle, and cry rivers til I fill it.
Have you ever seen a tear discouraged?
It's like my sobs are too crippled to jog the distance of my face
I guess you can say they're handicapped and disabled,
but for the sake of the children,
I will wheelchair these tears upon pages.
Call me the lamest poet ever,
or some type of Special Olympian whose whimpering
scrimmage from the heart but, never finishes.
It's our babies that finishes first
when they cross that flatline ahead of the old heads...
...aint that a false start when a child dies on the way to headstart?
I wish heaven would take the starter pistol from the devil and
let him play with the metal, "Russian Roulette!"
Much respect for those that rest in peace,
and those that resonate with this piece.
I wish the world were vegetarians so we won't have beef.
I wish cataracts consume my eyes so I can't see grief.
I'm so sick with earths crisis that I might shed a tear later,
you know, cry for the babies, and
stop being prideful and
cry til my eye is lazy like, "Christpher Wallace."
Maybe, just maybe,
I am a cry baby.

Spark from the emptiness
known as nothing yet the embodiment of everything
collision or combustion
simple an expansion of energy
my entity took on identity
intelligence in quest to manifest
rulership of the cipher
constantly growing I began showing
of my presence to come
his-story is one always being told
infractional fiction claimed as some religion
toll of division my decision swim swifter
show and prove how I arrived at the matrix
of the axis which shall sustain my essence
until I've taken on the knowledge to born form
of a being supreme
exit I from triple stage darkness
into the weakness which is light
where I with my might and duty
must right that which is wrong
showing and proving the strong
are those who are wise
and move with open eyes
to the power of the third
building and destroying constantly
civilizing the uncivil
most lose focus and fail to take notice
of what it is I speak
Black Man God lessons from Farrad
the formula revealed
that woke those that were sleep
not on a pillow but to the world
and Universe that has been theirs
if only consciously they claim
Black Woman my Earth
Far beyond the worth of the words
Bitch and whore
Queen balance of everything

Though she rises to no higher than
I who stands soul controller answer holder
And seed sower in her mental and physical garden
Fat her undulice and internal beauties
Like manifesting the union of the Universe's relation
Which is that which fills
Night skies the stars
By order of this Universe
Is the cipher complete.

RE-ALTERED BEAST

Push it to the limit and go hard living like a savage.
Where the wild things are in the wilderness of bad habits.
Although holding my own if I like yours I've got to have it.
Just like a dog with rabies I'm reacting unpurely rabid.

Savage meaning one who has lost knowledge of self and living a beast
life.
Let's be clear, the blind leading the blind with no idea of what right's like.
I am mentally Ill and my mind is plagued with disease.
I can't think right but got to hold tight because I know this ain't me.

Caged up and for no reason, I can't figure out how to break these chains.
Haunted at birth on that certificate enslaved by a name.
Through empty eyes there is no sight I don't see any equals.
Growing up learning from my T.V. to bring genocide Willie Lynching my
people.

Throwing bricks at prison houses the new plantations and homes for
slavery.
Tribal wars in our streets delusionally thinking we proving our bravery.
We've substituted the tobacco and cotton fields for a field of dreams.
Black rude boys ready to die giving red blood clots looking for that
green.

Living so high and willing to go toe to toe with the grim reaper.
Afraid to sleep I've not rested in years because that beast a creeper.
Even when I blink it's law that I keep one eye open.
Will I ever have the power to refine my state of Mind? Let's keep hoping.

Now enter the reality that I'm in control and master of my cipher.
There's no one to blame but me, so exit that fictitious viper.
I've got to own up to all my problems and mistakes I made.
Snatch the dirty sheet back off that bed where I laid.

They say that fire purifies, well I'm back from hell and feeling clean.
Feelin' like I just exited the matrix and true self is being seen.

It's clear out on the table now what needs to be done.
All praise be to the sons of man, each one teach one.

Just as the sun is the foundation always shine that light.
Respect and cherish your earth, plant and raise your seeds right.
Never let them forget who and what they are, they're born identity.
Leave the "N" word for which it applies; give it back to the enemy.

I also ask you to refrain calling our queens anything but their names.
Think about your sister, daughter, and mother that from which you
came.
If she's known as some out of wack character, remember she reflects
you.
Yo' son always be aware of everything self says and do.

Keep it positive and you can avoid traveling the path I laid.
Because not everybody survives to tell the story of the dues I paid.
To all the Gods, Earths and positive people of the universe, I say peace.
Heed the word of the brother from the Re-Altered beast.

Whispers to my soul

My silence is broken
I speak in a language never once spoken
Only I who understand me
I am mentally in a place no one has ever been
No footprints in the sand
Understanding the words that the wind whisper
As we converse what teaches
Humble rocks on shore watch speechless
Decoding the dialect that details life secrets
They cried tsunamis
After hearing the task given to Katrina
Not even a rock can visualize
Families broken into pieces
On the banks of the shore
I and the wind weep and continue to speak of disasters
How can one fathom the horror that happened to Haitians
Pray a halo over Haiti
The wind ceased its breeze for a moment of silence
As we strolled slowly across the calm ocean
Of Antarctica's thawed glaciers
Where polar bears clung hopelessly afloat mini icebergs
Again my silence spoke
What if the Mayans were right
The wind heard and blew
Life is just one breath.

M.A.R.I.E.'S KISS

Your kisses lead me to contemplation,
where visions of us submerge within elation (Remember?)
the wavelength called we,
sung in vibration seen sweet!?
Her kiss complete me with tenderness,
softly within the winds of her breath
do I confess,
my pure satisfaction found by her lips caress;
blessed were we who kisses like Sun and Earth,
Woman and Universe do I feel as I rehearse,
these motions of mad bliss.
My dreams create you nightly,
as my heart proceeds to fight me,
away from your love once held,
so I awake in pain daily to embrace this
lonely hell!
My memory of your kiss treads clever,
seems like we should've been forever,
but I guess fate has something better....
In store.
So I explore what I once realized with you,
in hopes of creating kisses anew,
but I fail to veiw,
A love like Gods kiss without you,....
Present with heavens affection,
and a smile held as my obsession;
So I dream,
"I dream," "dream" of us to relive love's perfection.

Places please!

Uha um, uha um, places! Please, everyone please take your places. The
world has been
patiently waiting for a reality, not the show. One must realize its evolving
powers will
flourish, once one involves every characteristic of itself.

Scarcity may promote bad health, but self introspection builds wealth
within the
contender. So before you decide to ride or die, consciously search your
heart, and see if
your pride is the drive behind the reason why.

Auditions were taken while you were shaking in your father's scrotum.
Grow up and
accept your place. Placating the man leaves you moved to take the place
of the
replacement.

Paste the word loser on your face as a face lift, because you're being
played with like
clay, and this ain't for play.

People choose fictitious roles in the presence of a foe, but little do they
understand---
Their modeling the deviant control of a naïve, pompous, nimrod with a
simple mind;
who's the biggest simpleton to undermine.

There's a narrow road, which has bolted many into an undeniable role; a
role peers can't
pressure, a pimp can't dress her, nor could a bully-bully a monster.

And being fake won't get you in the in crowd. On this road, being
mundane is strictly for
the lame.

You've graduated; you can make it through anything with a dream.

Recognize that you're in a **L**eague **O**f **S**upreme **T**hinkers. Who has been
taught how to
Navigate **O**ver
Mis-education while **O**btaining **R**ighteous **E**ducation.

Face it, its true you owe no one an explanation, but the most important
person and that's
you.

If you're chunky love it, If your nose is as big as Pinocchio's (minus the
lies).Be grateful,
and poke yo' nose in Wall Street door.

Where do you place yourself: Are you an independent thinker who has
placed itself in a
position to succeed?

Or have you been placed in multiple placements because you're placeless.
If so, monitor
your pace before I place you like a playmate in a playpen.

I accepted my place when I placed this pen. And as my thoughts descend
formulating to
words, actions and habits I practice;

Practically I'm placing myself before the director yells action.

BANJO

I'm wounded,
like beautiful music beaten & bruised.
No wonder my heart bleeds profusely through coagulated artistry &
strum harp strings loosely like un-tuned arteries.
I'm a poet, arguably,
like riotous noise be over docile harmonies.
Can you hear my chest organ seethe audibly
& my pulse beat silently against your eardrums?
The discussion.
The flustering.
No visuals-
My percussion blindfold open minds so the tangible can feel it-
The pain that is,
that dance so rhythmless like a ribbon blown by a tempest,
or a musician grandstanding with no tempo.
Can you dig it!
How influentually my pain is driven?
I feel like a mannequin with no mannerisms.
I'm a hymm in disarray, flung from a mechanical piano,
or an out-of-breath lung force to perform acappella.
I'm a prosthetic parody.
A harmony harboring hostility.
Pathetic aint it!?!
I'm just a clef left to labor,
entertaining inner pain while saxed upon a staff,
my demeanor sorta half-mast.
I'm a glass drum beaten into shards and pieces,
& I'm speechless like a composer gester;
I'm just an instrumental.
I'm a whisper like a toothless whistler,
or a tootless harmonica.
Please, no sympathy cuz, "NOBODY KNOWS"
that my pain is composed like, "Beethoven"
so, Please no symphonies.
Leave me be to bear this baritone of weight alone
it's fate, plus I'm a high note abased.

A prostrate high-hat.
I'm a sarcastic hand clap.
A bereaved finger snap.
I'm a crooner crying songs of despair,
but don't depict me as spineless cuz
I'm so inclined to lean on my trombone.
I'm a drummer boy with a warriors song that soldiers on.
I'm a bagpipe with no swagg.
A would be woodwind with no air.
Face it, I'm like a bassless bassoon.
An oboe full of woe who's afraid to face the music.
Oh malady!
I'm emotionally trebled like an erroneous chord struck,
or like a mournful horn blown amuck.
No wonder I'm stuck feloniously behind bars,
I must be a syllable flawed.
I must admit that I'm as brass as it get,
yet, I fret not like a neckless guitar.
See, I do me, whether in prison or free,
in or out of key-
A-flat or B---
I remain a cymbal at peace.
A lute with no strings.
I'm a lyric that don't lyre.
I kid you not, my heart is as acoustic as a tuba and,
I'm confused mentally as if I've been fiddle on the roof.
I'm as shallow as a cello.
I have fits and rave like a slave driven violin.
I'm a tune un-wanted and
according to the way I'm castaway, I must be an accordion.
This is my pedigree, my inner symphony-
Please, no sympathy!
This is soulfully between me and
this banjo on my knee.

Write about my life!

Paramount motion picture
I'm that token black guy in the picture
that just grin with white teeth
taking shots through the whole flick,
sick of the world, so I reinvent myself
with death and dope. Inner city broke black man
chained to hope or some sort of inspiration
or motivational speech with Greek philosophy,
that complex dialect, a slight slur, that gin
bottle bum, slum litter luggage. Some say I'm
scenery propped up to bring the ghetto rhythm
and soul.
I say I'm broke and cold,
sold to a higher cause by bias laws and bullsh-t explanations.
What was my flaws before the alcohol and crack.
My black face and this nappy hair that don't want to blow in the air.
I can be Cuban or Puerto Rican waiting for a train chain
smoking in New York, New York on a new port.
Still a n-gger, black and greasy as pork.
Abort me America or support me in court America.
Tell the Judge how I love to be the butt of the joke,
poke at me like you did in those old black and white pictures
where the perfect fixture is my dumb ass helping white folks with bags
or yes sir'ing my way to Hollywood.
Should a wooly wooden dummy get off your knee and dance
for a token.
"You ain't gon whip me is ya
sur cuz myz strangs broken and I'z hopin'
I'z could make a lil summin' extra to eat."
Beat it chump it's 2012 we gangsters and drug dealers,
petty street hustlers and senseless killers,
urban legends if you will.
It is art depicting life or for real.
I mean in black America does blood really spill?
Na'll we just trying to make money,
funny how prison population's sky high and that same

black guy fill the role.
I got a new dance for parole.
You expect me to violate it anyway,
so play with me.
Remember I ain't so bright,
I just might come back the same night.
That's alright, you can keep all the stereotypes.
I'll rather just sit here and write...about
my life.

Chicago Cubs

The wind blows heavily through this forgotten forest
Although some cubs may call it home
most of them end up left alone.
While Mother's roam in search of a better home
Pop's gone singing a whole new song.
Unattended with no guidance
some commit suicide.
Unaware of the danger that lies before them
lions lurking the land looking to devour anything they can.
Most "definitely" these little cubs don't stand a chance.
Scared and curious all at once
what could this be besides my lunch
danger strikes our young cubs - one by one.
"Product of a broken home"
yeah same ole song!
but if pop's stayed home
maybe this would be a different song.

The Understanding

L.O.V.E — can be tricky at times
that little feeling inside
when we're together
may only be butterflies.
Many of us mistake love for lust, or a big crush
never taking the time to look deep inside
you know, behind that disguise
that we all wear sometimes.
Because of the fear of getting hurt
from that last jerk (or) that sister in the mini skirt.
"damn"
Is this what's love about?
Sometimes I want to scream and shout
but then I realize that we were young.
And there's not much we could have known
about the word called, L.O.V.E.

DON'T LET IT GO TO YOUR HEAD

Hey baby, may I ask the question how are you living?
As a whole that question goes out to all my Black Women.
Let me sun this light so that you may reflect the wisdom.
Take it as you may and hopefully wise words spoken are good for the system.
Don't hear this with deaf ears even if you don't understand just follow me.
Queen is the Black Woman who is drawn up to her fullest equality.
Capable of holding the title mother of civilization straight from the earth..
Never-the-less by all means the supreme Queen of the universe.
Allow me to greet you in peace, be easy Queen.
I can sense it in your essence that you desire all the finer things,
but in all be truthful do you really believe you're at all worth it.
Don't let the sex and looks go to your head now, show and prove that you deserve it.
Calm down and catch your breath my intent is not to disrespect.
Know that you are a beautiful being ma, so why you acting like that.
In a way such as believing your looks are all you got going for you.
On the outside this whole world can see you're beautiful.
Carved out to the tee a living, breathing, walking piece of art,
but what's important here though is how beautiful is your heart.
Honestly your sex game may even be on point and extra hot.
There's only so many times though before that grows old on the block.
Not to mention the obvious dangers with that issue.
How long do you think that will keep a man with you
We're going to search deeper to discover what's on the inside.
So we can disband from your mind so called imperfections you try to hide.
I'm serious and know my women have much more to offer.
That's if she does not let greed, corruption, or low self esteem stop her.
It's all yours, and I'm not the one to say what to do with your body.
Respectfully what's meant for you and me ain't meant for the eyes of everybody.
You're the personification of self confidence, but you lack self respect.
Instead of prostituting your essence, place self in self check.

Whenever you are lacking and can't find respect for yourself.
How can you seriously find yourself disrespected by anyone else?
Looking for love in all the wrong places in any form that you find it.
The reason that love hurts so bad is because that love is kind-less.
Love self first ma, then you can go on to seek better days.
You have to learn how to choose and want better than the games you play.
Things may seem well for a while, you may even have a man spending dollars.
Picture yourself as a mother, is this the life you would wish for your daughter.
For how many reasons can you give that's worth the pain.
For what it is today it will be tomorrow and the next day the same.
Keep away from nothing leeching vulture type dudes and go for self.
Realize that self is a beautiful black queen second to no one else.
Be fertile as you rotate continue to grow and nurture for the sweet earth you are.
Allow the negative to exit the atmosphere and give birth to positive stars.
Share the light space with one who is to be your alike.
One who know the flesh while appreciating self's intellectual insight.
Fed with the proper knowledge of self wisdom is no longer mislead.
Queen I'm loving where you at now, but don't let it go to your head.

WHY I'M POETRY

I transcribe with perfect precision powerful enough to move mountains. Pragmatically promoting depth in thinking as words convey regal foresight foreign to enclosed lunacy!

Normally, normalcy lacks an open-minded approach, therefore I telescope mind matter in lines that bring stars to a page.

My purpose is to redirect the rebellion reasonably responsible for the lack of rationalism rampantly rendering rational thinkers rambunctious ramblers.

Today toddlers have mustaches and beards. Redefined diaper wearers that causes adults to think like kids.

The defecation that handicapped elevation links Huggies to Depends.

The pampers that pamper dependents who bring shame to the descendents of men!

In the beginning there was me.

God body!

Creations miracle!

though lyrical, blasphemy is not my intent, but after being breast fed my growth cultivated Eden in my head!

Eve was the day before I realized that Adam was me and although Lucifer was present, I had the presence of mind to undermine Judas and the insight to make right what John the Baptist intended.

The Messiah is coming and through my lineage maturation will be moved to a heightened state.

I am Poetry's essence!

My movement exudes it!

My crown proves it!

My pen is the Kings ransom and I bejewel sentences with prophetic messages that will only breathe when I'm breathless.

Becoming Lazarus through my lines, resurrected spiritually by the spirit of supreme potency.

I am a...

Paradigm
Often
Energizing
Tactical

Responses through
Passionate
Outburst
Educating
The
Receptive
Youth!

My **T**estimony **I**dentify **P**ersonal **S**olutions to the
Social **P**roblems **I**ntellectually **T**ranslated.

Hence, It's with a purpose that I spit Tips.

I salvage salvation through scriptures of worded philosophy used to impregnate the virgin virtually responsible for our victory.

My Ideology is ideal if the idea is to create rather than destroy.

I am Sire because I emperor my empire.

Cleopatra spoke me into existence and grant it, my thoughts are alien but I am an earthling.

Before I transcend I'll remain in this skin until I master this earth thing.

I dialogue with Venus only to find the meaning to the missing dimensions missing me.

My calling is light years ahead of most.

My transcendence transcended the outer limits but it won't be until I return that you'll get it.

In my demise there's a prize.

The proof of my existence will be eternalized in every volume of "Behind These Eyes."

Kuta's "OutCreye" encases tears of pain etched in blood to capture the weeping of sorrows sadness.

The Genesis of my genius is meaningless if I fail to utilize these lines to make my time on earth worth it.

Intricate introspection is an invaluable resource used to evoke the preservation of my Mother's distant voice and the dignity of my Daughter mixed with the integrity of my Son which polarizes the severe need of me and as long as the world is in need of me, I will continue to transcribe and verbalize serene solvents sincerely second to none simply because I am the meaning, the essence and the manifestation of poetry.

My conscious is talking

I'm searching for meaning
understanding greed
six feet from the edge and it's not a dream
hear the screams of a state prisoner
try to envision your world closing
those who know you say you lost it, it's all over
they sleep, I've awaken
tongue potent
speak the way God spoke, above all the rest
In my poems you're a guess
now drink gratefully
my knowledge is pure I seek faithfully
pray for thee the day I find what isn't given
since birth been in a blizzard
what's worst there's no ending
the air is thin, I'm breathing toxin in this wasteland
death in the face of a hate man
power is what he lust for
Bush prime example, destruction eat his soul like cancer
predicated the day he be white master, Hitler's reborn
torn from the wounds of Satan's belly
I speak with the wind such heinous tellings
as a student I understand, my soul it bare it
he who is lost by laws of land he fear it
neglecting his twins, soul and spirit
communication level like a wave in the river
out of place taught to hate and only self destroy where he live
sell drugs to the kids think like a boy not a man
the plan is simple, solutions to our struggles
words of Martin and Malcolm
love thou brother

My conscious is talking

the ending so close, It's here taste it
death in our faces confirming what is written

the signs and the symbols beyond the rhyme of this riddle
we lie to our children, everything will be okay!
they will never see that day, chaos among people
they birthed to do evil, give birth to that sequel
baby Satan he like nine months away
the stereotype is race and they paint this face
black as sleep without dreams, sun without gleam
define life without means
and Satan will do the rest
training wheel rider since birth been behind
your life been defined 3/5 of a man
they plotting on our seeds and they scheme in the whisper
you're not focused you're victim, your future their system
Is economical slavery for brothers behind bars
and prejudice hid itself behind these unjust laws
my conscious is talking beyond the words of this poem
and they cursed this earth and I'm writing their wrong.

My conscious is talking

My brothers I sit and watch you humble yourselves
but respect for a man is more than his wealth
we got seeds to look after
I weep through this chapter
our past is the truth we been through the disaster
let's lead by example
perform what is great, believe in your faith
and God will be with you
please pass me the tissue, your brother is crying
let us iron out our differences, together we shine
no more what's mine is mine
you eat from hands, you eat from my plans if I should ever blow
God as my witness, I lie to you not a friend to a friend, I'll rot in this box

My conscious is talking

Application

Some women think
all men are suspect.
Like we the weaker sex.
Like we only get geeked
for sex.
I expect and respect
honesty.
An enemy of neglect
replenish me with the success
of sincerity.
Do me the courtesy
of believing in my fidelity.
I'm not talking mutual funds.
I'm talking mutual trust.
Invest in us.
Inspect
my personality
see if it's enough.
Or else you might get
your heart crushed.
In the dark
whispers of poetic sparks
light your life.
I know what you like.
Red roses and moonlight.
My verbal eloquence
imposes on your life.
I suppose it's your
intelligence and
conversational wit
that makes you my type.
We can exchange information
or swap applications.
I don't want one nights.
I want one wife,
the fun type

who gets hyped
when it's time to communicate
her needs
and don't believe
the prison stereotypes.
I'm not a down-low brother.
Or a low down buzzard.
I don't come from a broken family.
I know my mother
and I ain't too thuggish
to admit I love her.
My worth ain't defined
by past mistakes.
Ambitions that last are great.
Renditions of Mozart
my heart is Gothic art.
Ghetto Shakespeare
my tragedies equivocal
to King Lear.
I got the capacity
to love,
to learn,
to grow.
So, please done prejudge.
Although I love
a woman's hips
and pretty lips
it's
more than physical.
I don't want a shallow romance
or a tepid infatuation.
I want something
that's going to last
beyond graduation.
Beyond limited education.
The edification of two souls.
Since you want a brother
to qualify

I hope you ain't too fly
to apply
standards that's high
to yourself.
As far as an application,
I don't need
a judge
to referee my pedigree.
I get my references
from my past lovers.

Understand me...

I battle me uncasually
Because the casualties
That I so causually caused
Caused me to cause an effect
That I still regret.
An hour ago I checked my astronomical clock ...
The readings read 1 and 9 ciphers.
I spit because I spent an eon deciphering the engraved grave of graven images
Imagined by the imagination of a public image who was made in a splitting image
And perfect likeness of me.
This is the astrological wilderness of my own mind
Where I spent time indefinitely-
Indenting these declarative sentences
And my repentances formed in the form of informed knowledge
Acknowledge by the god who give me knowledge of me.
I Self **L**ord and **M**aster-
Masterly mastered the masturbating mental mentality
That often ejaculated
Subatomically
On the physical pages of stablized reality.
So tell me, "who carry the vocabulary and don't vary very voluntary
More than me?
"That's rhetorical"!!!
It's self-evident that I am immortally born and perfectly sent
To perform the strategic strategy surgically needed to reform
The immoral abnormalities that done became the norm.
And normally I'll formally address this situation more informally,
But this ain't rocket science conformity.
This arithmetic.
And if you can't add this up...
"Then you ain't spit'!!!
I spit because vibrations vibrates the assassination of **OutCreyes** that burst out

Like cloudburst of teardrops that remain dropping inside of ancient souls.
I strolled through the holy scrolls while in a hellish place called purgatory
And bore witness to the forgery and forged full force ahead
And unfolded the mental folding of hands and handed it back
Right and exact to the sons of man who were deaf, dumb, and blind to the actual fact
That they are the suns of man.
I hearsed these hamitic curses
Unearthed these mental verses
And rose to the surface.
I am "the one" within the 144,000 who you may know as the chosen few
"I chose to choose myself" !!!
This is why *I Spit With A Purpose.*
This I why I walk through universes conversing with the perverses
Who thirst for wisdom's knowledge
And I acknowledge that the American college
That we call universities
Be converting these
Ancient prophecies
Into pseudo philosophies
Agnostic atrocities
And ya'll be jocking these
Aristotle's and Socrates'
But I be mocking these intellectual hypocrisies
Whose off springs be product stocking these original seeds
In projects and cell blocks from greed.
"God say let it be and it be's".
So I bleed internally to spit externally
For Gods of eternity to arise and manifest this biblical reality...
Psalm 82 defines self actuality. And in all actuality,
My morality is obligatory to explore and destroy the subminal wars
Criminally waged by the criminals who subminally ignore
Universal rapport of mathematical justice justly adjusting
The balance unbalanced by the chemically imbalanced.

RIOT WITHIN

Injustice fills my heart with fierce protest
as thoughts of streets in peace displeasure deep
the spirit breathing air that moves my chest.
My feeling crushed by every endorsee.
They notice not the innermost distress
of signs my psyche embrace for appointees,
and one that reads: "I HATE TO LIVE OPPRESSED"
by smiles with mocking dispositions bent
on faces full of lies, exuding white.
While seeing red, my inner residents
explode on avenues to damage sites,
so Molotov cocktails they throw at length,
which burst with speck of flaming glass at night.
A car is rocked until its weight upends
as people hang from traffic lights and scream
their curses vandalize American
dreams,
and plan
loud rebuffs.
No game crowds cheer.
Boo the place where tough
police in riot gear
stand by buildings burning from
the gasoline solution spilled.
Guards disperse the mob with flashing bombs,
but damn, if only everyone were killed.

21ST CENTURY TELESCOPE

My prophecy is apocalypse, for hypocrites
pre-historical prediction, pre-conditioned
prepared me to expose high society
like Ho's, not pimpin Ho's, but ozone Ho's
space station Ho's and global Ho's
I play with ancient technology, comparable to street philosophers
spitting historical rhymes-
my telescope, got me aiming at the Sun and Moon
wondering how the eclipse shine-
spiritual signs, combining the atmosphere and gravity
inside my palms-
Mother Nature was artificially impregnated
on the eight month she had a miscarriage
so they named her fetus, "Katrina!"
mama, FEMA need a telescope! up close in my scope
the government claiming, "their broke while hanging us
from trillion dollar deficit ropes!"
mathematical voodoo, subtract 12 from 20, equals=
"the President race of 08, get it? (08)
twisting revelation 2012, with my mythological, metaphysical
poetical style-"
I slay frozen brain cells, bodies standing still
I bring judgment, upon private gold corporations
blowing meteor holes into our cosmos-
please, explain why the oxygen flow so low, at ground zero!?
Lord, send us a super hero!
mortal men forgot to protect the kids in the ghetto-
I never saw a friendly helicopter...police chopper
news chopper, the devil running through the hood
shooting choppers!
people packing pistols, grenade launching missiles
equals, billions-
senseless killings, brings countless body bags-
My prophecy is apocalypse for hypocrites
pre-historical prediction, got me searching for the truth-
teardrops falling in the form of nuclear bombs-

peace talks is sterilized, being crucified for telling evil lies-
bodies injected, society is secretly tainted
programmed for a Jihad, Yahweh and Allah!
I'm seeking Yom Kipper daily!
at birth my wings were clipped, now I'm struggling to
duck these demons packing clips-
I petition hypocrites, discharging 'em for perjury
abnormal hypothesis, demoralizing your mental leeches
multiple characteristics collapsed and collided, my conscious
and sub-conscious, causing me to see life after death
in parallels
patriotic state of minds, are revolutionized Kamikaze militant groups
spooked and hopeless, I can't help 'em I'm focused!
high altitude, my latitude is 90 million miles reversed
from this Earth, solar system so hot, this is astronomical!
the Moon has potholes, compared to Pluto, atmosphere is
what I'm told-
metamorphosis, I'm seeking paradise but blinded and paralyzed
by Pandora's blood jewels- colorful gems
zodiac signs are beautiful signs-
reality play so virtual in my telescope
macrobiotic laboratory test macroscopic techniques
It's hard for me to be optimistic-
the astronauts flying intoxicated
there's no space here on Earth, earthquakes (49) million people homeless
(15) million orphans, struggling physically, spiritually for food!
Lord, my eye rhymes revealing inhabitants, prevailing through these
diluted times-
destiny, she blessed me with several biographies, psychologically
my philosophies, grading hypocrites thesis, a paper full of feces
now ain't that diabolical?
NASA stole Saturn's ring and propositioned Venus
in hopes to be engaged and live on Mars-
rebirth of a new star
style is unidentified, liquidated through poetic scrolls-
historical words, smoking words are legendary-
21st century telescope, up close, my vision is clear, reverse prediction
pre-condition, prepared me unveil life, in closed captured-

capturing biblical signs under the heavens
these are my modern theological concepts
causing a combustion of awareness in the mental of those who lack
awareness-
ps,
"you cannot capture time, you can only mold your existence around
existence.

"21st Century Telescope"

This everything I have
I mean ain't none of this sh-t half so don't laugh
it all adds up just do the math
1 idea I decided that I'd follow
2 have her a part of me
3 parts of me, mind, body, and soul
4 ever I mean even if I died
5 deaths and arose for a
6 breath of life, I still wouldn't see
7 lifetimes where I'm finally in front of the
8 ball that I feel I'm behind where I wanna put a
9 under my chin and end it all and just be the
0 that I feel as empty as without
1 moment with her, true she may not have a clue
2 exactly what goes on with the
3 of me, mind, body, and soul, that is as we sit in
4 walls where they seem to be alive, me hearing
5 heart beats, mine and theirs with
6 hours passing like seconds in chairs taking
7 stares at the same clouds as they make like hour glass
8's let's get one thing straight
9 never equals that of
10 like I could never be
1 going in a 0 for the sh-t she do
2 the average man making him talk to
3 different people to get
4 points of views like being interviewed on channel
5 news
6 in one hand is
7 in reality the hand and the half dozen with
8 times I've told this to myself with a
9 mental metal issue pistol put against my
temple, so take it for what it is
and all equals up to
1-3 is only half of the 6
sense I should've used to
determine to count on the

love of her view and see that
bullsh-t add up to bullsh-t
whether it's in a rodeo
or out a preacher mouth in a pulpit
and this is
bullsh-t!

Nauseous

I feel like my dinner plate is loaded with seafood
from the aftermath of the (BP) oil spill
after watching news reporters report ill news
of another inner city youth being killed.
My stomach can't hold anymore,
my inspirational advice has fallen on deaf ears
and being discarded like vomit hitting the floor.

I've experienced a tingling sensation rush through my body when
I hear rounds of glock 40's, within the circumference of 40 blocks-
It's absurd; my central nervous system has used its last nerve
in attempt to revive me from what I heard.
Summed up into one word, Salmonella!
Poisoning me with your ecoli
trying to distort the vision of my 3rd eye.
It's a lie, like the homie Boo once said,
you are only 'Kids Killing Kids', the modern day klan
with black hoodies and black gloves on your hands.

Trying to regurgitate what I distaste has left my esophagus swollen,
while intensely witnessing you cry like a baby
over your baby-mama not being sentimental enough on Father's Day.
When in fact, in the past 90 days
all you gave your 9 year old Son was a pair of J's
and taught him how to throw up the trey's.
be real!
You in too deep, a low down negro and niggard
whose entourage is full of nimrods that brag on their man's cars-
calling girls bitches,
but wear their pants sagging down showing their britches.

Naturally nothing positive is manifested from becoming a victim of
recidivism,
coming back through these doors like they're revolving with rhetoric as
ism, digest this realism!

Haven't you realized that your friends aren't your friends and the phrase
"Ball Til' You Fall" is the end.
You fell like Goliath from David's sling shot---hard and fast!

But my E.S.P. tells me, you can't stop, won't stop
even though you got popped-
I'm sickened at the site of the same faces returning back
like they left something, fighting the same ole cases,
chasing mundane wages,
with your last glass chase it with ass
because your full of it, and I'm nauseated behind this bulls—t.

Guess what I herd…..sheep!
just as sheer as s--t is steep, I will shepherd my people
to keep them from being led to the slaughter
come hell or high water.
Word, to the wolf called, society-
not one bleat shall be lost
silly me,
I forgot about the anxiety that causes extreme nausea
in our communities-
It's like I've tooted a vial of virile buffoonery thru my nostrils
then puke what appears to be mucus-
                Ugh, I'm feeling nauseous!
and sorta narcissistic to the bulls--t I've witnessed
like the triple (A) down grade on America's default being lifted
they fixed the debt ceiling short of a few billion
while on the Southside of Chicago, the Ikies raised the death
ceiling-
senseless killings-
                Ugh, I'm feeling nauseous!
From seeing visions of falling children playing, "Your It!'
outside their bodies, forever playful prisms-
I'm sick of nigga's claiming to be men
only known by what gang they're in, nonentities
who swear allegiance to leaders who leave them in limbo
with nothing but a number and pseudo notoriety-
now a steel box holds your body in detox, that's not sobriety

this is the influx of what humanity call just,
us stuck in the middle like Malcolm, X marks the spot
three meals and a cot-

Ugh, I'm sick of this S--t!

Like the stench of piss that lingers in gangways
that gave way to the gun play that murked Shorty
in his three-piece-suit on his way to Church-
Let the choir sing hymns, while his Mother screams, "Lord Why Him!"
Cursed be the planet for not bursting in tears
and crying rivers over these earth crisis,
or rain down fire and brimstone on the wicked
like Lot did in the Bible-

Ugh, I'm feeling nauseous!

Forgive me if I discharge my disgorge on paper,
but I can spit what vexes me from the gut for pages
can you smell how decimated my hate is?
I'm throwing up paper trails like front pages paint pictures
of domestic violence being predicted-
This has to stop!
Like the killing of innocent children,
the usage of drugs, gang bangin' and drug dealin',
let's promote the Love that's missing
so that we don't have to listen to the screams of Bay-Bay
and them offspring's
being carried away by sirens.

Hieroglyphic Motion

My motion was written in truth forbidden,
to eyes wide, yet swelled and smitten;
History becomes the victor legacy,
while I become customized in religious drapery,
as wrists flick to make ink stick,
I become impure and used as a trick.
but for those who acknowledge this,
and free the minds of those who follow this....
Path away from the serpents hiss,
There is bliss!!!
Found in the image and form of my divine composure,
emitted from an original mind with no closure.
"Justice is Truth,"
measured in my every follicle of hair, bone and tooth...yes!
My stance is timeless in its infinite expression
of youth.
So you who gaze upon me in mystery,
understand that my design is life mastery,
which proves that God is no mystery.
So visually,
I am the symbol found in every form,
from the "Big Bang" to the elemental chain storm,
restless though in motion like wise lotion,
I be and become born!!!
Hieroglyphic Motion.

Breathe Brother Breathe

He said man shall not live by bread alone; it's the historical events that give our strength
life. Brother, you're not by yourself; life's journey is full of lessons... And with positive
counter reactions you'll receive blessings.

So accept this oxygen... Deep breath after deep breath, for what little life you have
left!!!

Since the fall of man, a chemical agent has been designed to create a dysfunction within
your nervous system. Yet have you mustered all your courage to emerge your nerves.
Fight this fight to the bitter end, as if it was the fight over your sins.

The whistle has been blown, the bell rung, and the stop light has changed (green).The
spirit of Morgan Garrett is echoing your name;

admonishing you of toxic fumes that will potentially fill your lungs like a balloon.

Meanwhile, the fallen are spiritually testing you—

"HERE IS UR GAS MASK! --- BREATHE BROTHER BREATHE!!!"

Life coaches around the world are calling for a 20 sec. time out, after watching you
pleading for air.

While being submerged in money, sex and drugs. Your vigilant eye has said goodbye to
this age, now is the time to turn the page in your story book.

Brother no matter the color, you have seen and/or read enough to know
enough is
enough. Wake up and step into the shoes that were personally designed
for you.

There's no excuses, we have men who made it because they change the
cards they were
dealt. Who were raised by a single mother with no government help!

And have been the butt of many jokes before graduating Magna-cum-
laude and becoming
somebody. Not your ordinary somebody, but a loving husband,
somebody's brother.
Somebody's cousin, somebody's dad and somebody's friend.

Imagine this being the beginning of the rest of your life.

The end is here, I'm sharing this air with you because of what I fear. One
does not have to be Nostradamus to predict your future.

Truth is, truth doesn't need a witness. In your life time you have
witnessed boys
believing their men because of their age (21 yrs. old). Factually, age don't
make the man,
man make the age, a man with a mature mind and purpose.

Take advantage of what you have today; with less than half of the
technology we have
our forefathers paved the path. Don't give up yet or become a loser,
within this great land
we believe in no surrender and no retreat.

Salute yourself, when you're look in the mirror, you're looking at a man
that posses the
heart of a lion. Form an alliance with yourself in order to keep breathing
life's breath.

This is the day brother you receive your break through, so remove the oxygen tank from
your home and find that brother whose lungs are not so strong.

killa

Ay, yo, I'ma killa
unreasonable, unapologetic, I said it & I mean it
no inbetween wit this shit.
I'm the N-word where words end
we don't work it out wit words, that somethin' the "nerds" did.
I don't converse,
I just level the first person to come thru the door,
& I couldn't care less whatever he came for.
I'm lashing out
I don't even know what I'm mad about
I just wanna stomp somebody til they pass out
& end up somewhere in the joint ass out, AIDS in
I dove in the deep end no thought to wade in.
That's why I'ma killa.
My decision makin' process don't process the punishment,
I jump in the dark water not knowing what's under it.
And I love frontin' when it's nothin behind it.
They say seein' ain't the same as being unblinded,
see what I'm sayin'?
I don't even know if it's a way to illustrate understanding.
Then again, I don't care cuz I ain't never had it,
if that was some sort of class I prolly never pass it.
But why would I want to?
I'm just "doin' me" even when I follow the leader
that is until I do somethin' somebody else think of,
but until then, I'm still a killa.
I'm the bastard that grew up & passed it down,
it being negativity & everything it's wrapped around.
This is what you thought it was in every single way
I am what you think I am & this is my resume.
I killed King & helped bring slavery about
I'm on the rise right now in the craziest amount.
Ask the teachers if they see me
cuz I'm mostly what they students see when they watch tv
a bullet can't kill me, but it's said that a book can

by now you should've figured out exactly who I am.
I'm a killa, a.k.a. stupidity
wrapped around ignorance underneath hostility.
I roam gated communities & ghettos alike
I'm wherever you never find peace or settle a fight.
I'm where intolerance meets misunderstanding
I'm a bully, if I can put this simple & candid,
I'ma killa.

MY LIFE CRY...

The wind whispers secrets between us two.
My feet warm beneath the wet, sandy floor
as waves dissipate upon the lake's shore.
I see gulls and the sky is a clear blue.
and I notice no one but me in view.
A heavenly ray beams from the sun's core,
yet my heart feels no solace, only sore.
Wishing it were easy to start anew,
I hopelessly dream of a perfect life
with all the luxuries minus the strain.
I try to wrestle back tears cause by strife
and all the held-in agonizing pain
going through my emotions like a knife
until finally I let my eyes drain.

Sonnet

Concrete Tears

The concrete cries justice for the selling of co-<u>Cain</u>,
making people un-<u>Abel</u> to regain...**balance!**
Here's the challenge unchanged,
so as to conquer the brains natural effects,
customizing society to adapt to thee insane...**predicaments!**
Allowing prisoners to remain lame—**"So Silence!"**
with the evidence of truth in attempts to mislead the youth,
with uncanny provisions governed by a twisted view,
correctness is a cloud that appears blue.
(transparent that is!)
Looking in the sky without a clue.
As mysterious scenes illusionate days with dreams of....
religious voodoo spoken from a pastors bastard seam.
To profit fiends submerged in desires steam.
This is the cry of the concrete!!!
From the miscalculated steps of drunken teens,
dying without finding self. (and this is thee esteem!)
Dictated by television screens;---eyes wide and worldwide (mothers scream).
Blasphemous incisions to the third eye,
overdosed with pain heard from the concrete's cry defying,
empty automatic shells collected by police forensics as they apply,
pressure to an atmosphere blended with sighs,
stimulating hatred to spew envious lies.
In a barrel where all the crabs die;
pulling each other to the bottom with no means to explain why!
Through the smoke from blazing guns do we emerge...
over bodies of slain sun's left traced to visualize,
by crowds hovering the perimeter of yellow tape.
Where fatal cases lay embrace by the concrete's face.
Petrified with disgrace and left crying!...."Concrete Tears!"
It's far too many of you dying!

Window Pain!

As I sit here in the bracket opening of this wall, I'm forced to reflect on the pain I have endured over the years. My pain isn't that of open display nor have I succumb to the marking of my body with ink. My tears are not tattoos, and time has permitted my soul to be bruised.

At the old age of 74, the tears that ran down my cheek in 1974 have left a permanent stain on my face. So I ask you, baby, don't take your father's place.

It's inevitable that I warn you of your path, in the beginning he concentrated on the math. I've watched him from this window frame chase what they call street fame, with pretty cars and designer clothes made by stars.
Thus far, the game has always been the same. Due to jealousy and envy he was slain, and the authorities story remain...his street life was to blame.

Ambulance and police sirens became funeral home music to my ears, what is it going to take for you to adhere; It was a horrible sightseeing you being taken away for taken another man's life. By the age of 20 how could you be going through this twice, fighting for your life when their trying to give you twenty to life.

In my heart I know it's not right. I tried to give it all, I prayed, I paid, even put up my house for your liberty, and this how you repay me. I'm all alone, on my own, as a praying grandmother, where did I go wrong?!

I've set in this window so long people claim I came with the ADT alarm system. It's too painful watching the future of America's youth go down the drain. I have lost my hair, gained some weight, tears don't well up in my eyes the same, but never will I lose my faith behind this window pain.

THE WHALES BELLY

I've anchored my penmanship near the piers
where the screams of my peers
voices were last heard.
Forgive me if I submerge my emotions
too deep into the depression of this Ocean.
Sea, I'm hopelessly floating on hope
off course and off coast without a sail
hoping to echo locate Gods offspring
like whales and Dolphins.
But turbulent winds blow kisses that tosses
the serenity of my offerings,
and since my marine skills ain't Navy Seal
my craft bow begins to submarine...
...I'm drowning...! I'm drowning...!
Or am I dreaming!
dreaming of being harpooned and
left bleeding on a beach called F.E.M.A.
I dreamed I had a brief affair with a Sea Urchin name Katrina.
Am I a merchant having nightmares of me surfing Ocean waves
just to savor the remembrance of this man made mermaid?
God forbid...
...I wouldn't be so afraid
if I was he who was brave enough to walk on water,
without argument
I'm beating the waters with the faith that sunk Peter
now I'm in the belly of the beast with these SONS OF ANARCHY,
which in essence vexes the vegetation of my inner vegetarian,
now my good Samaritan craves meat,
so I speak proverbs of PROJECT PARABLES to the meek
to make obese the anorexia of my humanitarian.
From a sea I remain stranded alee the reams
of this recycled elm
via violent storms
search the Holy Book of Poems
9-19 v 70: knowledge was born.
I was spawned in Romans Times

but it's time to flip the script
and spit with a purpose in cursive.
It's time Romans no longer have access passes
To freely roam these passages
To passionately pass them off as their own.
We've come into our own
And are prone to kick asses with the same ashy limb
That Kunta Kente kicked rocks with.
I spit with the sass of kissy lips
And build with the bricks that blow with the glass & lumber
From the Atlanta church bombing.
I stand barefoot in slums where bums be,
But could still hear the drums of my earth sons far
East of where my heart beats.
I live that I might give these gems back to the fields
Fondled by the middle fingers of so called forefathers
And if I had the tools to forage deeper
I would give B.P. (black people) back their oil rigs…
'behind these eyes' is where the oil spills,
My swamps of New Orleans is eternal
I'm burning in the inferno looking out The Window of "ROOM 197,"
"spitting to the heavens,"
Adlibbing my past miseries until my mysteries
Adhere to Adams Apples.

The whales Belly

HIDDEN THOUGHTZ

My closest friendz, are my hidden thoughtz
A world beyond this world, look around-
We're bleeding and pleading for Repentance-
My third eye shedz tearz, producing acid rain,
Breakin your flesh, traveling through your brain-
Programing, I'm aiming and delivering holograms—

Reflection, bright flashes in form of
Small pieces of broken glasses-
Containing substances of evil gases,
Returning ancient her delusional war crimes-
Crushing, Alexander's not so great
Hellenistical concepts-
My footsteps, are envisioned as I walk
Throughout every ghetto; I diagnosed
That "Poverty" is a product of a twisted tongue,
Being guided by planz lackin truth-

Schemes, trading physical war games
Kidnapping, Birthlandz and lablein'em insurgents-
It's critical, I'm giving you access into a world
Of one of OUT CREYE's Prophets-
I'm still feeling the second life of Lazarus,
Even back then they said he was cursed-
All because his corpse never road in a hearse-

Cemetery visions, got me lingering
Over "SEAN BELL's" grave-
Wishing I could reverse the bulletz rippin through his flesh-
Deep inside my soul lives a possibilty
While hoping and praying for my seedz growin
Through these high weedz-
Fallen leaves are transformed once hittin
The pavement-
Reincarnated into wondering soul'z, strugglin
And seekin, eternal refuge-

Rehabilitation is a damn dream!
It's all about packin bodies into cell-houses
And get that cream-
I awoke from fighting demons, I thought
The wallz was screaming-
Grown men hiddin and crying, "I told you I heard screaming!"-

My closest friendz are my hidden thoughtz
A world beyond this world, look around-
We're bleeding and pleading for Repentance!

A Conscious Thought

Amnesia

Do you remember a time when there use to be strong black men,
Who built Holy Kaaba's and Pyramids with strong black hands,
While the strength and power of the sun shined down upon black and
beautiful skin?
I remember!
I remember a time when the stars would align,
And black men would decipher the symbols and signs
That were sent down from the ONE who created us with illuminated
minds.
I remember our noble elders,
The kings and queens who ruled over majestic lands with a love supreme,
Everyone knows about Egypt, Nubia, Mali, Songhai, Timbuktu and
Kush.
But there is so much more that's been untold,
Thousands of years of glorious history,
That too few know.
Don't you know that before there was brown, tan, red-bone, high-yellow,
olive-tone, or white,
There was BLACK!
And genetic scientist will tell you that!
On the day of His creation,
The first man had earth-tone (black) skin, tight curly nappy hair, and dark
eyes.
The DNA,
The biological and physical characteristics of all of todays so-called
"Races", "Ethnic Groups", or "Nationalities"
Were passed down through the ages from our common ancient
ancestors.
So even if your hair is blond
And your eyes are blue,
You still got nappy roots.
The oldest human remains ever found belonged to a black woman,
Whom they nick-named 'Lucy',
Whose remains were unearthed in the highland mountains of Ethiopia.
And anthropologist will tell you that!
Through the method of carbon dating,

They have estimated these remains to be tens of thousands of years old.
I know the truth.
I will remember and I will never forget,
That black men and women were the first to set foot on every continent.
I'm talking about strong black men,
With strong black skin and black nappy hair.
That's who laid the foundations of the earliest civilizations.
This is something we all should know,
We all should respect,
And if you know, never forget
The land we call Africa is Eden the Garden,
The Motherland, the Birthplace of all mankind.
MAMA AFRICA!
You gave birth to civilization,
Culture and dignified royal kingdoms in the far too distant past.
MAMA AFRICA!
Your fertile soil produced the fruits and vegetables that nourished the
first black man,
Who fathered the first family that grew into a clan,
Then divided into different tribes, and lived in scattered towns and
villages,\
And then spread across the continent,
And eventually,
Throughout the world: North, South, East and West,
Into Arabia, the Middle East, Persia, India, Asia, China, Japan, Australia,
Indonesia, the Islands of the South Pacific.
Even North, Central and South America,
The sons and daughters of Africa dispersed throughout the four corners
of the world,
To settle and develop new towns and villages, holy cities, temples and
monuments
That even today defies imagination.
And archeologist will tell you that!
But time and chance and circumstance
Has forced all men,
Because in the successive migratory waves of Africa's children into other
lands,
As they traveled farther and farther from the nucleus,

As the climate cooled,
As the days grew shorter,
Down through the ages,
Generations after generation, through the filter of time.
As skin tones gradually changed,
From BLACK to brown, to tan, to red-boned, to high-yellow, to olive-tone, to finally white,
As skin tones changed, hair color and texture changed, and as eye color changed,
One thing has always remained the same,
We are still the sons and daughters of ONE father,
And ONE mother has always cherished us close to her breast.
So you see,
Everyone has had a golden age when knowledge and wisdom,
Science and medicine, education, technology and spiritual enlightenment
Has flourished.
Everyone has had a chance to shine under the sun,
Although some seem to have forgotten where we all come from.
Every so-called "Race", "Nationality", "Ethnic Group", "Culture",
Every complexion of man, in every age and time,
Everyone has had a chance to shine.
The ancient Nubians and Egyptians built pyramids all up and down the east coast of Africa.
The Arabians can boast of the Holy Ka'ba,
The most ancient house!
The first structure on this planet for the worship of one God.
The Ethiopians and Yemenites can boast of being The Lands of the Queen of Sheba.
The people of Mesopotamia (modern day Iraq) created one of the (7) seven wonders of the ancient world,
"The Hanging Gardens of Babylon".
The Persians had mighty kingdoms led by Xerxes and Cyrus,
Who is mentioned in your bible?
The Alamitos, Sumerians, Assyrians, Acadians, Moors, Masai, Zulu, Mongols;
The people of China, Cambodia, Thailand, India, Sri Lanka and Ceylon;
The Vietnamese, the Maya, Aztec and Inca,
All of these people built great civilizations with temples, monuments,

pyramids,
And empires that still amaze researchers.
Even here in North America,
The natives of this land had dozens of tribes
And lived peacefully amongst themselves for hundreds, maybe even
thousands of years.
The Lakota, Cheyenne, Seminole, Hopi, Apache, Mounds, Anastazi.
Blackfoot, Sioux, Cherokee, Shawnee, Pawnee, etc.
Every people, in every age and time took pride in their accomplishments.
Maybe it's the insecurities in man that provokes him to pride and
arrogance,
Which gives birth to such evil racism, prejudice, discrimination,
segregation, oppression and genocide...
I don't know.
But I do know this, no so-called
"Race", "Nationality", "Ethnic Group", "Culture" or Complexion of Man
Has a right to glory over another
Because really, really, when you begin to talk about BLACK HISTORY,
In all actuality,
You're talking about WORLD HISTORY!
Because we all came from BLACK, or have you forgotten that?
The most progressive and forward thinking
Genetic Scientist, Archeologist, Anthropologist, and Sociologist
Will tell you that there is no such thing as race,
Except the HUMAN RACE.
This whole issue of racial superiority is a fabrication.
It's a lie!
It is a form of reverse psychology that was invented by those,
Who for whatever reason,
Felt as if they were in some ways, inadequate.
And in order to inflate their own self worth,
It necessitates that someone else must be put down or brought low,
In order to raise themselves up from their perceived position of
inferiority.
But there is no superiority of black over white,
Or white over black.
There is no superiority of brown over olive-tone,
Or olive-tone over brown.

There is no superiority of red-bone over high-yellow,
Or high-yellow over red-bone...
We're just people,
Men and women,
And there is good and bad in all of us.
Even though some choose to deny,
And prefer to believe a lie,
I know the truth.
I will remember and I will never forget...
If We All Came From ONE,
We Are Still ONE!
One God, One Goal, One Aim, One Destiny, One Love!

Written By

E.-M. Hicks Jr. A.K.A. Abdullah Ilyas El-Mandi Hassan

Chapter three

Unfortunate Urbanites

Gunshot blast...
screams definite,
so sharp they shatter Plexiglas.
Feet trample over notepad and bus pass,
old man watch school kid
get murdered as bus pass.
Mayor blame gangs
for youth killing uprise.
Must of forgotten Feds rico-ed
Gang leaders in 1995.
Illinois Senator
win presidential election,
Governor allegedly auction Senate seat
while we seek direction.
Criminal elements elevate among civilians
as well as political echelons
who delegate what fate and
who become pessimistic epsilons
Disenfranchising Americans become
A franchise that,
Americans can't seem to resist.
Resemble rural militias and pro—white supremist while,
rich money elites deem the extreme to persist.
Seek deep money funneling schemes to redeem
low self-esteem towns,
prison boom bloom profound,
incarcerate unfortunate urbanites born in a game full of less ups and too
many downs.

MONSTER

Since the creation of Frankenstein,
I'm the biggest accomplishment.
My development is self-evident on all continents.
I was suppose to be just an experiment
inside a lab where scientists' main intent was to invent
a monster to weaken the strength
of a black people's percent,
so the dire descent that I represent
wasn't meant for "civilized environments."
But yet, I'm prevalent,
Disguised as a resident roaming the streets,
an accident longing for freaks and people in poverty,
who enjoy being on folly and keeping me company
until I opt to ravage their bodies
because I'm a greedy creature.
I leave you with skeleton features,
walking the earth like a corpse deceased in dirt.
I sneak upon you when you're least alert. Incognito,!
so I don't appear to be a vicious beast at first,
just another citizen who pretends to be a heaven—send
so I can blend in with different woman and men
and make them my friends by offering sex and heroin.
If they accept--
that's when I win, and after they've finished the sin,
that's when I grin.
It makes them mad.
I get under their skin
and forge a union within.
That's how I become half human
and travel the land at first hand.
To further help you understand,
I can be a woman's husband.
Beauty and the Beast loving and sharing a bed.
Don't snort. I want you sharing needles instead, henceforth;
I got a lady helping me spread.
An escort who exchange me for bread.

Then smoke a Newport--
one pack to the head.
I kill Dracula's dead.
I'm a monster no bigger than a needle—head.
A lethal virus you can't stop with meds.
I'm H.I.V.
The Loch Ness has nothing on me.
People hate to confess I exist in he or she
because I'm a guess unwanted like a refugee.

REMEMBERING ME!

Reality is really the state of mind
where reason ridicules fallacies and
fictitious thoughts brought into fruition
by the same temptation that persuaded Eve.
Once bitten,
trust becomes rotten to the core
and lies begin to feed on the remnants of reliance
causing a lifetime of enmity, which created enemies of lovers.
Two hearts at war all because a promise unkept
swept from mind like spoken words to mimes.
Your word was bond before it was found to have fractures
from the smiles you cracked towards our love-
unfortunate cause love was the foundation
that created the duplex of two souls so complex in nature-
Oh how I hate how we lost our estate
all because you bought into deceit and planted seeds
too deep for he who trust to reach-
But like the grief, the rain gone come
and the seeds you planted gone see the sun,
see, when that hour come I'll be that flower
and I promise you'll be remembering me.

I AM!

I stand still while slowly moving to the destination before me, on my
back I tote a load,
knowledge I've gained and a story to be told. Speeding while slowly
approaching the
fork in the road. Carrying the struggles and heartaches of Kunta Kinta,
embracing his
strengths and forgiving his weaknesses as they made him Toby. Only in
their eyes did they
see such a name, that whip they used to beat him, for his weakness it
takes sole blame.
In another lifetime we established the underground railroad and it wasn't
for a train truth
be told. I embody the fortitude of Harriet Tubman, as she led those to
freedom with
creative song. I embody the fortitude of Truth as Sojourner, as she
expressed her
struggles through words, I embody the same burner that our brother Nat
Turner used to
destroy plantations. I embody the fortitude as John Brown. A willingness
to sacrifice,
while helping others gain ground.

In another fight I stood alongside Huey Newton and Fred Hampton, I've
seen and
fought against more bloodshed. I've stood with fist in air, gun on side,
black gloves,
black hat black jacket, as black men full of pride. I stand as a black man
on the rise.
I've marched through Montgomery and Selma with Martin, I've felt the
rocks, I've heard
the dogs, I've felt the spit of those who counters we sit. I've marched for
peace and felt
eternal grief I fought with Medger in his racist home, I was there and
they tried to kill
me. I was near when they assassinate Brother Evers and I've seen the

ghost of
Mississippi and how a life can be taken so quickly.

I created the black star line with Marcus Garvey in an attempt to keep
our people from
starving. I am that imprisoned fella, I served those 27 years with Nelson
Mandela.
As the story goes further with more hateful things, I felt every blow
those racist cops
gave to Rodney King. I rioted in the streets of L.A. full of frustration and
pain as a white
jury acquitted white cops for doing what was seen. Allowing loud cries to
go unheard
while giving them permission to do the absurd. To go unpunished for
doing the seen,
gives little hope for justice for those acts unseen.

Profound and perversed acts towards Abner Nuima, wasn't enough to
do, explode 41
rounds of hatred expressed their goal towards Brother Amadu Diallo. I
even felt the blow
to the face that they gave the old man in New Orleans.

I embody the fortitude of all these people and until we as a people
embrace our strength
and the strength of our ancestors, we will continue to stand still while
slowly moving to
the destination before us, we must stand together as a people and take
hold of the powers
that was given to us at birth, stop waiting and bust first if worse comes to
worse.

I am....

How You Thought This Wouldn't

Hieroglyphs on thrones
mummified bones
still got the world mystified by erected stones
onyx and copper tones
Egyptian warriors singing songs
sharpening mental swords colliding in cerebral combat
conversating on the cosmos not fables nor parables
cause that fiction is terrible
religion is division and
don't ever make people one
just creates confusion making slaves of free thinkers and
provides a little security to those who lack discipline and maturity
some'll hate me surely cuz I comprehend my chromatic combination
is from a long line of sages
whose contemplation created my creation
let us make mankind, why not we made sunshine
periodic elemental chart are increments of my mind and heart
though I puzzle those who ponder how my mental is a vortex
transmitting perfection through my cortex
7000 B.C. existed the real Rolex fiber optic technology
concealed in Homers odyssey
cuz my people move modestly through master mind movements
like telekinesis and aeronautical time travel
Ezekiel seen the wheel and his mind unraveled
why you think the people destroyed the Tower of Babel
the landing tower for universal visitors not aliens
like they now claim with the mind game
making many lame attempting to regain and claim
the return of the ruler
that's why they bow down to the reminding black rock
of the greatest stock known as God,
Ignorance to abide behind lies
many tried to hide but here's the end of the ride
where I tell you what will happen from what I decide
this planet name earth upon which we live
will be caused to cease to spin 1,0371/3 miles per hour

simply by my power causing this 6,8 extilliontons
to be devoured every hour
all those who has open mental eyes will rise
while those who remain 85 won't survive this drive
and forbid you a truth concealer cuz when you cry the cry of the calf
I won't hear through my knowledge
how you think this would end
coming from the lineage of men.

Imagination

I thought I saw your reflection in the mirror,
but when I turned around you wasn't there.
I experienced the bliss of your touch,
and smelled the scent of your hair.
But again, my imagination had made a fool of me.
I imagined me and you walking in the park,
me holding you close to my heart.
As we walked in the park, it suddenly got dark.
And I awoke protecting my pillow from harm.
So I ask myself, "am I going crazy?"
"no"
"hell no!"
I'm just missing my soul mate,
my lover,
my best friend,
I'm missing you!

My Life

Conceived in Detroit
raised in Illinois
Holy City is what they call it
born to a crack addict.
Raised by the rules of the streets
wondering when I'll see six feet deep.
Bred with hustlers-groomed by killa's
now what's the odds of me being a doctor or lawyer?
Chances are a victim or parolee.
Cursed from birth and never knew it
but somehow, someway
I manage to still be here.
Family members and close friends have passed
and yet I still remain.
Is it luck?
No
I don't think so.
I think God has a plan
and he is waiting on me!

Breathe

I been chasing wind running after my last breath
Since birth
And all I had to do was just breathe
Exhale see the signs in the road
Align my goals and just breeze
Forward towards whatever I desire
That ignite the fire in me I be
Therefore, I am the light within the fire
That ignite the spark you see
Even in darkness I illuminate
I architect and inspire
And envision even higher
Until divine signs make my mind raw substance
That my life can hold on to
With this formula I solve all solutions
I add or subtract what matters
And give the prototype, then bring the blueprint to life
To illustrate a divine vision with the transparency of water
To purify the blind
As I walk through the valley of the City of Death
I shall embrace my destiny
Inherit the Earths constellations
Let nature take its course to where I am free
And intradependant with thee
I been chasing wind and all I had to do was just
breathe.

So Unkind

At this stage in the game it's safe to say life ain't easy and everybody plays the fool.
Simple as it may seem there will never be just one set of rules.
You will have yours and I will have mine he'll have his and she hers.
Although we were born speaking one language it feel like we never have the words.
How has it come that now a day we just can't communicate with one another.
Coming from a friend's point of view we're having more problems than lovers.
Forever so close but constantly going through emotional games with these changes.
Treating life like furniture on a roller coaster ride and always rearranging.

How did we come to this a point where you're now making me promises?
We're better than this you don't ever have to spare my feelings just keep it honest.
This prevents us from being in a situation that we could've avoided.
I'm not asking you to do anything especially if you can't afford it.

Look, listen and pay attention. we became friends before anything.
Meaning you should hold this conversation well in understanding what I mean.
Whatever happened to us there was a time we use to be able to talk.
Now you're avoiding our usual pleasant conversations like I'm one to stalk.

If there is something I've done wrong I ask you to let me know it
You said you had love for me and this is a hell of a way to show it.
Maybe we should start over as I take this time to reintroduce myself.
It is me that same dude that you never compared to anybody else.
Patience is a virtue, but I've already been waiting much of my life.
I'm asking have we come to the end or is our future still bright.
Just take the time to think about it we've had a great type of history.

All in all I'm missing you and it's hard to feel as though you're missing me.

Let's not twist these words or leave an opening for any other misunderstanding.
I'm a grown man and not about to cry over this it's not in my planning.
If you're satisfied with how things are then I'm cool with how they sit.
Being that things may not be on point with us let me know when to say I quit.

It's all good and well understood we all may have our issues.
We can go a different route and you can let me know what not to do.
For the moment I'm the one willing to keep initiating the contact.
That willingness is something to fade away because you're not willing to holler back.

The hardest thing about any of this is the fact of not knowing.
I do think of you often and pretty much still care how you're life's going.
It's not like we have bad blood or had separation do to bad terms.

We're just facing situations where we have to live and let learn.

By chance I still hold a place in your life, continue to hold on.
By chance if there's not let me know and I'll be gone.
Within these few words I may just as well be crossing the line.
That's only in an effort to figure out why you must be so unkind.

The Crow

I met the serpent on my way to refill the Holy Grail with wisdom. Landed I upon his back to behold his visions of war and spiritual collision.

Natures cataclysm amidst the waters where we spoke for hours about the struggles for power.

Realizations in times composure of mental vibration, revealed when nature created an opposite for means of self elevation, yet to be pure, one had to become impure upon the tree of damnation.

In his slithering revelation I beheld the attempts of many to destroy its destiny, scaled with uncertainty, he made the waters ripple a reflection showing the best in me.

Tempted, I was at this beautiful vanity, when he coiled with swiftness and aimed to damn me.

Sensing the threat and yet the density of realism, I opened my wings with talons wide to thwart off his biblical prison.

Releasing the cup to avoid his bites, hell fire flashed forth a remembrance of my cause of flight! Taking his head with might, I beheld a prism of light.

And by identifying each spectrum in its own right, I retrieved the cup of eternal life.

Full of wisdom and freedoms elixir emitted from the divines mixture, carried I the crow, back to life's victor,

The Men of Night!

Ultraviolet

Bi pass the ciliary processes
and vitreous humor,
enter the half lunar optic blind spot,
a sight dot will blotch the retina,
my optic scope lesser.
Reversed spectrums in sections subjugate
bifocals that lack focus,
your vision is impaired,
optical nerves and retinal artery's ensnared
rendering your eyes hopeless.
Severed ciliary muscles and suspensor ligaments
collapse corneas, pinching your scalars
in various predicaments that oscillate
rigorous irritation.
Making vacant eye sockets concoct phantom stimulations
rogue revelations are open invitations
for the words I recite to become visual demonstrations
in dimensions towards demographics far more graphic
than any syndication.
I'm sent to nations
with tenacious metaphors
that never relent never before
in any situation.
I write grammatic glaucoma's
through parallel realities in singular form.
Run through commas brainstorm
through commas where my verses perform
focal points sharper than crosshairs
in sniper scopes,
serious enough to devote seekers undivided
insight to what I write that's in sight.
I write me -see-
that explains why the average eyes
can't see me -see-

I'm just too bright

Lothario

It wasn't that
I was playing games
or what I was saying
contributed
to me being vain.
My life convolted and insane.
I was trying to maintain
from the strain
of a dead-beat dad
who was conspicuously bad.
Although discrete
in between the sheets,
he was ridiculously sad.
When he left,
I was dizzy
like I had jet lag.
I ain't even been on a jet.
But I use to jet
when it was time
to take my relationships
to that next step.
Technically, I never seen
the "Stairway to Heaven."
I broke bread
with womanizing brethren.
Ciphered with seven.
Didn't mean to tear you apart.
The fun, passion,
and looks from your heart
had me charged.
Like a factory of hybrid cars.
I treated you
like you was made
for me to discard.
can't believe you
viewed my as your God.

When it was time to depart,
left you deceived and scarred.
Girl, I put yo pain
inside these bars.
Seduced by bliss,
the touch of my fingertips.
I kissed you with cheating lips.
My wandering eyes
disguised by my intelligent wit.
I used your tears to shower with.
Brushed you off with
a flick of my wrist.
Rationalized it
by saying we didn't fit.
tried to pass you around
to my friends
like that sh-t was slick.
A twisted dimwit.
It took me getting my heart broke
to understand love ain't no joke.
I hated how it felt
to scream to God for help.
Growth made me love myself.
So I say to you,
I have changed.
Forgive me boo,
for the heartache and pain.
Didn't mean to ignite a flame
The fire inside a woman's soul
can never be tamed.
Humbled and ashamed
accept this poem
as a token of your beauty.
I'll always love you and for me
I hope you'll feel the same. Truly.

Chapter 23

The Lord is my King,
he reign upon all things,
his word is supreme.
I the human being shall not covet for jewelry.
He makes me lie down in green pastures,
the absences of my earthly father doesn't make me a bastard.
We as God's sons and daughters feast on manna as he provides us.
I seek, Tranquility & Serenity!
He leads me beside still water.
Arid and near dehydration,
he restores my soul.
Dancing the way David did, I'm souled out.
Desperately panting on the road,
he guides me in the paths of righteousness,
for his name's sake.
I vow to be great
like the number 23,
33 years is enough to attest to my existence.

List this....

Yea, though I walk through the valley of the shadow of the Chi, (Town)
I will not be shy, distraught, or fictitious.
I will fear no evil.
Gun shots will not scare me.
Politicians will not sway my vote.
My faith will compel me out the boat
for you are with me.
Your Rod & Staff comfort me
Bathsheba will be Bathsheba...
Consequence will be given if I decide to meet her.
But the filing of Chapter 11 or 7 is neither.
You prepared a table before me in the presence of my enemies.
So in essence, the end of me is the beginning of me.
Anointed oil drips from my forehead,
thus giving me the go ahead.

My cup runneth over!
Blessed be my community, family, and meeting place.
Laced with skills like Nimrod, the mighty hunter before the Lord,
surely goodness and love will follow me
all the days of my life.
Strife with the world will be resolved when light conquer darkness
I'm encouraged to ignite a spark equal to the brightness of the son's.
I honor the heart of the psalmist.

And I will dwell in the house of the Lord forever,
And ever, and ever, and ever!!!
But only if Chapter 23 is a part of my endeavors to be perfect.

Verbal Assault

Faced with constant dilemmas,
being pushed to the point of
no return.
Strategic moves to place me
on the other side of this fence
has been my only concern.
However observing my surroundings-
I sometimes feel like I'm alone,
laughs, giggles, and wearing house-shoes;
this place became a comfort zone.
It's sad to watch the complacence
of this new so-called man,
being that I'm cut from a cloth
that was taught how to take a stand.
I'm viewed as a man that lives in the past,
I'm the product of a dying breed-
taught to stand firm, and not kiss no ass.
Paradoxically speaking-
you're actually no different than me.
Even I'm told to bend over
to let them look at an ass that even I can't see.
It's time for us to all wake up-
so we can all be on the same page,
not strength in numbers, but in knowledge;
then we're able to set the stage.
However, right now I don't think we can-
nor for the lack of better understanding,
built mainly for the lack of a better man.
Our history reveals that we're all sons of Kings,
forcibly removed from our lands.
Knowing this, and still you do nothing;
I just don't understand.
I guess I'm a one-man band,
who's sound falls upon deaf ears.
These may be just words to you,
but inside I shed tears.

I shed them for my true soljaz-
believe me, they know who they are.
Even though the world will know us in time
because we'll all shine like stars.
Until then be patient,
and always remain out of sight-
the time will come when we ask;
"have you ever danced with the devil
by the pale moonlight?"

Dazed and Confused!

I struggle to maintain a certain level of consciousness
about life. I don't mean to depict a victim
but I fit the description in a system of a madman's device.
I'm in a living vice, pressured by
self preservation and black political power's preaching advise.
I fight to see another day in this fenced in society,
where the prey wear blues, chewed up
by over reacting overseers while we pray the blues-
cripple and abused like: old slaves in a trade
where the profit is chopped up by greedy flesh merchants
working any man for any purpose. Murk his ego,
hurt his pride...f--k his life, he 3/4's of a man
in his government's eyes. Devise political platforms
to perform forums for hate-crime suits against Hitler,
Mussolini and Kim Jong Il, as if my country
never was once them that killed, by shotgun blast,
strangulation or legislation or any other sick twisted mutilation
that brought about the worst in my nation.
Been taught how to bob and weave from a seed,
my southern ancestry conceived through ruthless battles
of out stretched legs and forceful penetration
raping my great great granny screaming to God
this demon depart without further ripping her young insides apart.
Now how am I suppose to feel about that,
I don't even really think she understood that she was black.
She related it to the pain and that abusive thing
just keep coming back.
She gave birth to babies that gave birth to babies,
that gave birth to babies and they gave birth to misconceptions
that feed itself on the breast of deception
and dead hope, my current condition is sickening,
poverty stricken, we dead broke and the promise of be
fruitful and multiply is a dead joke...we dying out here,
and that ain't nothing to laugh about.
My pride's all passed out and my judgments full of doubt.
Got me in the world moving chaotic like, the chains are still

tangled around my ankles, limiting my mobility
while I angle to be free...as if that's physical.
It's a mental state and I'm an illegal alien escaping the bad land
of pain and despair to share in the bliss of this mental prosperity::
I proudly display my family tree's prosthetic limbs.
I know I came up short of them, but we bare the same seeds,
so Yah is sparing me. Remember, mental prosperity?!
Yahweh for ya'll that's slow along the path and need me
to pick you up and carry you the rest of the way.
Exodus 3:14, 29 words spoken to open those the closest
peep! anyone of ya'll can be Moses,
and the called is always chosen.
They all suffered in some form or fashion: that's deep!
My passion is transmuted into speech,
incarcerated in tight confines counted 3 times
morning, evening and night.
So I write according to a precise cycle.
A 7 or 360 degrees,
A cipher or 29 in some circles, so I'm never incomplete.
I speak with my ancestors when I can't seem to shake the
feeling of defeat.
I'm doing push-ups under these people feet.
And it makes me stronger but they think I'm weak.
I make them reap the wrath of my ink pen or my art pencils,
tongue or any utensils: physical or mental, carnal or spiritual.
I know who I am and where I come from,
I got 9 major spirits orbiting me, I'm my momma's only son
and I ain't burning out no time soon.
I generate enough energy to telekinetically move everybody in this room,
but they assume I'm an ingrate like X can't get things straight
and I'm suffering from some karma driven fate making the fake
more faithful than proof that's why history don't expose
a violent rape of our roots my hands ain't dirty cuzz I'ma convict
I stay digging for the truth.
We the fruit...we food, and give this to my seed and
anybody else that's starving to believe we better than this...
thing that society perceive us to be,
obviously I got the Spirit of God roaming in me

and we be on a spiritual plane.
When I explain how, Godly it be to be psychologically free.
They can't keep that monetary man power
and honorary man shower most get devoured
in critical thinking hours we lost most of ours
shackled on slave ships that don't make us cowards, when
we disrespected God we sinned inward, but paid
for it outward
that's what got us devoured.

Remote Control

If rewind wasn't only a button on a remote control
or standard feature to some console
and could actually fold back the fabric of time
and find the first frame we spent froze
in the pose that curled our toes
right there I'd pause I suppose
just to feel the rush of our adrenaline in harmony
hungrily calling we to be
the beauty that causes creations to crave existence
and stars to travel distance in desire to shine
in a simulating spark like that of the look we share
when we stare at one another
if only fast forward could actually fix the fractures
created from us being separated
I'd be adulated
to sweep away a falling tear from your face
before it begins its race and
beside you'd be my place
In my mind where these things play with torment
as price I pay it's strange to some this day
think in such this way
if only they say as they lay
technology could alter reality
love would not be a fantasy and
something they all could cop
I just smile of us on repeat
and press my button on the world to stop.

Testament – Reverse

It all started with the apple
Not the snow white bite; this is no fairy tale
This is the seed of the fruit of temptation
the catalyst of apocalypse from the garden to metropolis
from eternal life to prospects of hell
It wasn't the bite but venom that poisoned our thoughts
It was the curb in Adam's rib that bent him to deceit
So you see she was the apple to his eye all along
the rest is history, blasphemy, mass murder, God name used in vain
This is B.C. gangland where messengers speak the word and flag a sign
Nations collide and towers fall and ground zero is just a revelation
While disciples suffer the Pope share and enjoy the fruits of war
lives are lost over rites of passage
And each verse is a violation by the commandments of God
The soul insights passion, so politics in religion makes extremist
We're suicidal time bombs with holy war beliefs
holocaust lost, and heavenly expectations
You should never fear God but crucifixion is the example
and they showed no compassion for Christ
When the Saint's come marching in, communion is commorated
and the black sheep is the sacrificial lamb for which there is no salvation
Man is the author of confusion, chief deceiver
painting the picture of this porcelain pigmentless pilgrim
to portray God
Then expect for me to submit to man because he got blond hair and
blue eyes
where's the demagogue in this debauchery to oust the devil in disguise

SELF---IMPLOSION

I collect my thoughts because during the implosion I misplaced focus.

The exchange was made but, the benefit of the swap wasn't conducive to my solidarity.

Time traveled way too fast and it blew portions of me in directions unattainable by the suction of my vacuum.

My whirlwind bypassed the gathering process anonymous with hurricanes which leaves me to believe that my typhoon was symbolically a storm for fools.

Why am I questioning mission impossible when admittedly, I am mission impossible!

I can't conquer my spirit if my soul is the victim of defeat. I can't battle the ghost of timeless mistakes if I fail to confront the bully of decision.

So who do I blame for the flawless victory bestowed upon me during morals combat?

As a mortal I can come back from a fall but, if I skydive from life's plane without a parachute, do I blame the pilots ascension, not to mention, I was the fool who paid for the fuel.

My descent was complete when my body met the concrete. now I sit scattered in pieces trying to collect my thoughts because during the implosion I misplaced someone sacred.

During the fall I screamed but couldn't escape it. What a tangled web we weave when street lights are shot out and the victim becomes the thief.

Oftentimes we struggle to survive but imprison ourselves in straightjackets trying to be free.

The power of thought can build monuments but an idea slept on is similar to a sand castle in the rain. Beautiful when it began but melts away just the same.

Secretly I am God's genius, but Satan's puppet on a string. Muppet baby to ill things, but the invisible man to what matters.

Now I sit in silence debating my fate with fleeting consciousness.

Come back to me! is the recurring plea but the more I plea the more guilt that's attached to me.

I wonder if I'll ever be whole again, but until then I will continue to collect my thoughts-because during the implosion I misplaced me.

His garments are tattered, ripped by the resistance of the wind. Through elements he has reigned, casted by divinity-- knowing not the nefarious presence that was seen in him...He has fallen.

Struggling to stand, he experiences something he cannot understand until this moment--pain.

Through the blood trickling down his leg he realizes that he's no better than those he was placed beneath in the beginning of his perfect existence.

now he is me.

Staring into the soulless windows of men he never knew, he finally understood that through his carnal conception he was lost from the beginning.

In the grand scheme of things he was set out to embark on a journey with broken wings, so that it would be impossible for him to rise above it all.

was this his fate?

Deliberately stripped of his divine essence, forced to walk a path to which he was not accustomed; hated for the warrior he had to become. Battered and confused, he still wonders why he looks to you for guidance, knowing it would all fall on deaf ears.

all he has is hope.

Is it by any fault of his own? maybe he's digging so deep that he's barely scratching the surface.

His imagination could just be getting the best of him, or perhaps it's all just a vivid dream.

Can't Let Go

Please listen closely
this has control of me
not me control of it
I mean how could any hands lay
hold of a soul and cause the artery to
know and a heart to pulsate with
such a profoundly profuse passion
while also causing a pausing
in its pace or glow upon a face
eyes glazed over as if higher
than heavens height weighing the pressure
of a feather in zero gravity
so sweet it causes cavities in the cranium with
deliberations in demented delusions of suffocation
being satisfaction suicide is a sure summons for reaction
truly fatal by attraction
never wanted to die until considering
the cold clutch that I
without it would have to continue on
day through night I despise the oxygen coursing
through my being night through day
lungs burning with pain shuffling my feet
sniffling from the rain of reason
simply let it all end than ever try again
is the one feeling I stay fighting
for I'm glued to promise of love
and this you now know
the reason I can't let go.

Picture Perfect!

Can you imagine a professional painter's process when creating the
Perfect picture...?
In the beginning he's perplexed by a vast of notions before the premise is
manifested
through his mother's influence.

Oh, how he would love to paint a picture of perfection of the woman
whose arms he
rested.

As he scans over the many colors of paint, he's overpowered by the
Oprah effect.
His brush dips itself in the Color Purple;

Sophie's power to overcome comes to mind. He's impressed with his
choice he decides to swiftly paint a pair of drapers using hues of purple.

Hence, displaying her money, power, and respect!
She shares her life with the world, even from the point of a little girl.

With holiness in her heart he allows gold to ooze out his brush.
As he precisely shapes her throne along the right side of her King's
throne, his thoughts
drift off to home.

Surrounded by statues of prideful African animals, she's facing her
patriarch.
While a reflection from the sun rays highlight the glow within her angelic
face.
Her voluptuous lips compliment her permeated joy.
Her symbol of sovereignty takes the place of her motherly love

Perfectly made for a Queen the painter paint's gems at an angle where its
brightness is
unbearable.

This Queen's Queendom has been tested and prevailed.
Even the painter's stroke with the brush is impeccable to the touch,
when dealing with a picture so perfect as such.

The painter pauses before taking a few steps back; he could now visualize
the authentic art which came from his heart.

THE SOLITUDE OF MY HEART

No freedom's mercy in my one man cell,
just the quiet solitude of my heart
submerged in silent misery like hell.
I have spent days with a psyche torn apart,
ravaged by regrets in my chest too far
and deep to reach and heal with any herb.
So I know my mind's eye can see scars.
Nor can anyone correct what occurred
in my past life except me with words
I choose to restore my lost sanity.
Then from loneliness my body emerge
ready to meet with all humanity.

But more important is my peace within.
Without it I am just a tortured man.

Sonnet

Subliminal Phrases

Praises bound to subliminal phrases,
blind in 3 stages,
where defeated wars became waged with no wages,
blank pages!
Continue to turn as misdirected rage burns,
souls learn where minds yearn;
in spite of strife's pressure,
we become released from gravity as the world turns.
So in the mist of darkness
I decided to spark this,
heavenly sunshine while
the worlds watching from afar mark this,
universal beam spirit child,
gamma ray supreme, God style,
the objective dream as relative bliss seems
wholesome and handsome!
worthy of praise and some,
my subliminal self becomes known as the crown is shown,
wisdom approaching my throne,
shaking my bones to the truth in her song.
Bound to her….I praise us,
All hail!!....Subliminal Phrases!
folding from the depths of paradise
that my mental chases,
infinite traces of black faces,
whose racist? We'll misplace it
with longevity beyond the perimeters
of never where never erases
the basis of basics,
as seeds embrace it.
with eyes wide and stomachs empty,
my teaching is simply,
spoken in a place where devils tempt me to pimp thee,
for the sake of riches,
I was told to rise above bitches,
like M.O.B.

thrones before Bitches
my temple itches to open its doors and listen,
to the power in my position,
praise and admonition to the righteous mission
taken without bitchin,'
focused with no twitchin,
phrased up as my subconscious is raised up!
praise us!
the most why, the most high!
Evidence of divine man in light of the physical eye!

The audacity to hope

A latchkey kid
consistently kicked around
by economical indifference:
concentrated poverty.
The branches of bigotry.
"United States of Amnesia."
Constructed
with a constitution
of stillborn sentiments.
Bridges of hollowed hearts
march
down aisles
of shattered memories.

"Your Pyrrhic Victory

I tried to call you today-
once again I couldn't reach you.
Even tried to convince myself, "it's just me,"
though I'm starting to
believe my suspicions are true.
Respectively you've said you'll never leave,
once again I've played the fool-
and wore my heart on my sleeve.
A sane man would admit that
too much has been invested,
but I'm beginning to lose my mind-
telling myself I shouldn't stress it.
Please tell me I'm wrong about you,
so I can play this with precision;
because I don't want false pretenses
being the bases for my decision.
It's so obvious as to how you make me feel-
I would've thought that by now,
you'd know that the love I give is real.
Reminding myself that I'm a man,
I try to keep my emotions in check.
For you I've neglected friends and family,
can you not see that I'm a wreck?
lost in a pool of confusing emotion,
at times not knowing what to do.
Although one thing is for certain,
if this charade doesn't stop-
sweetheart, I'll be the one leaving you.
It's not a choice I want to make,
but I have to take a stand.
You already know I'm a man with pride,
and what you're doing is forcing my hand.
I understand that this separation
can bring about heavy strain,
so if leaving is what you want to do
then be an adult about it

because I'm too grown for these games.
A relationship is only as strong
as its communication,
once thinking that you really cared
being that "love" was your so-called
motivation.
So for now I'll bring this to a close,
and of this there will be no mention.
now you have to make a choice...
choose me-
or the man with you right now
who has all of your attention.

The Lone Star's State

Radiate through space and burn bright
from millions of miles away display discernable light
but I'm a far off star on a stark night, so it's like,
I'm not even noticed,
even by those celestial bodies that's supposedly closes.
My plight seems hopeless, but I don't give in I give more
so for their every one orbit, I did four.
Still, no responses that resemble a retort
it's as if my efforts at effervescence are only for sport,
but I burn brighter, rather I turn nova
and whatever foolish pride I had I turned over,
in turn my return from the ice giants is a cold shoulder,
like I'm a lone soldier, separate from battalion,
I feel crossed out like the Pope's cloak and medallion
so I stallion on an power through like Zenyatta
try to find the answer to my quandary I gotta...
From light years away they only see me as I was
So It'll take light years before they see what I've become
and what I've become is now reflected in my starlight
because what I was before was far from star like
I'm just hoping somebody notice before I go super nova
and my gravitational pull is black hole-ing 'em
because then I'm back home with 'em
no longer exile,
until then I need help just walking this next mile.
But back to the right now I feel so distant, like the length of a galaxy
and can't really tell if this is real or a fallacy
I just know that man ain't never travelled that far
I think the outer space created an inner space
and to make the distance up I need an attempt to enter space.
According to the "Big Bang" we move away from each other
I wanna reverse the polarity to save each other.
I feel like Andre, 3000 miles away
but I don't wanna be an outcast I'm proud to say,
I wanna make it back to my solar system to console my sister,
follow my father and hug my ol' Earth,

meantime they got me on a cosmic soul search
because to end up lonely you have to be alone first
and I'm trying to avoid both, the former and latter
and so do I star search to find a star worth its matter
because the fact of the matter, when matter factors in
It's what matters most or your matter is back again
I set my Onstar so my travel's navigated
so that now a-lone star can be a planted populated.

Shattered into a billion unbondable pieces
is that which I once called the
cryptic security code of my sanity
how did you invade my identity and
explode my every imagined idea
of the idea Queen
I have yet to answer such a question
so I quest on to know and enjoy the internet
of your intellect
building by linking on texting line after line
on lined e-mail
your sights are truly a web sight
I promise with all of my might
to move slow as a virus as
I up and down load into your intricate system
I know my disk drive is a server
I just hope you don't overload and crash
cause I'm your on line for line
mental mainframe anatomy frame cracker
computer hacker.

My Mother

The Virgin Mary was too scary to reveal
to the masses as Egypt.
The Kemetian land that gave birth to the mental expression of Jesus.
Every grain of sand is lifted when we return
to the promised continent surrounded by eyes burning
in fury because we've learned!
Envious of our birthright to infinity and prominence, disgracing
dominance because his-story is blurry when discerned.
The saga signifying the sagacious races,
with glowing faces of concentrated light and gleaming!
Anointed the sight of those blind and burning those dreaming,
from the pressures unwanted and daunted; so they taunted
the bitter hands shaping time to stand again,
bawled in fist as grown men!
The vengeance is dealt in righteous blows from blood filled pens,
beyond hypothesis and geometrical degrees of wind.
In love we begin to cease the rule of disease,
Three pages away from judgment day's end, so take heed!
Because prophetic, tears flow onto city streets as single mother's
fall to their knees.
Apocalyptic visions seize the village in unbelief because there's no relief
to a plague carried by the seed's mentality.
Holy morality or Herod's victorious fatalities?
Anciently modern casualties!
spoken by the pain of every prophet who left foot prints of wisdom on
each side of the equator.
Praise the mother and they still will hate her! (but I love her!)
Torn from a womb to foreign to remember,
to the children of Israel as cold as December,
"I brought you out of her!"
"I'm real!"
And so is Mary; "remember?!, Egypt?!!
I am your father and you my children are Jesus!

It ain't finished

Ancient westernized Asian philosophy
my chi is pronounced che'
because you may mispronounce Guerro
with Guerrorro
and these over confident battles are over dineros
I got the spirit of Masai warriors, I'm invincible.
My image is impenetrable, vintage like an
Andy Warhol stencil. I ain't trying to convince you,
my life fades with grades of depressive grays and blacks,
I'm a introvert so these shades kinda raised me like that.
See steel sharpens steel.
Still I'm volatile at times, I cut cause I'm sharpened
a shark in high waters like Al Sharpton and them,
I ain't saying I'm him
or Jesse or Oprah or ole boy
a political thespian
desperate to be seen in the next biggest arrest he in.
Or maybe he's a she and she's a lesbian
and she's a talk sh-t show host that
hate black men only to date white women
or she discuss racial topics with white men on CNN,
play the third party
protecting the system instead of the victims on black in America-
we all got the treatment whether
it be right now or back in America
but back to America.
How could we ever speak of peace
in the middle East
when we don't even have a piece
of peace in the middle of city streets,
at least the police
could decrease the madness
it release on us halfway
So we can crease a pathway
to bury our deceased decently halfway
and if we possibly make it halfway

prison take it the rest of the way
where we lay stranded stacked on top each other
like naked cargo,
and our slave vessels are immobile penitentiaries,
the Country's blood vessel's
a pen full of native black -entities where the scars show.
I'm from Chicago
where the beast wear blue
and they jump out vessels
pistols blazing, shell cases, hot to the touch of skin.
got us duckin' slave masters, paddy wagons, bull pens--
there goes slavery all over again.
I'm calling master...Sarg or Leut, or Warden
and these just ordinary men, who's job are to keep
me physically and mentally locked in.
Do all acting parties know their roles?
Probably not
but should they spot my flaws
knowing just how they sin.
Blasphemy Son of men that laugh at me.
Ye shall be cast down to the earth
like the beast and the least shall profit,
expect a prophet, the way the world
devour Yahweh's children in the flesh and blood
consuming feast.
I ain't gone say I'm a Saint or an Angel
or neither, but I damn sure ain't gone let the system
portray me as a demon either
when our people were screaming evil at the top of their lungs
and these were the lyrics our ancestors sung.
Now we're being judiciously hung
with the bench kicked from underneath our feet
and the jury better not say a word
or the Confederate conglomerates'll have that ass wrung
for a single noun--
(na'll pardon the body)
a verb are a slur or anything heard uttered from anybody
cause anybody could get it, got it.

This is political science at its finest
and the findings is society's rotting carcass,
this cocky mutha I need to fall back a minute
I'm stuck in it, just like you in it
it played out the way they meant it
don't think for a second, since it was a minute
it's history...It ain't finished!

We Hail From The Center Of The Sun

As masters in molecular cosmic construct
with mentals that move masses
tune into the conflux
we are no mystery
simply supreme entities
3rd optical retinal radiators
often labeled alien trinity
we speak laser linguistics
with precision to curve intellects through craniums
and birth vision
10 hertz to the 23rd speed
we travel in
but those who claim Ken
its plancks we move in.
We are the evident evolution of evolvers
the visit-ores is what many cult-lures, have called us
we strike in visible truth light
to ignite sight photoelectric
like life breath being brought forward
by atomic celestial collision
and no unseen fantasy.
God can grant wishes
organisisms nebula clouds plasma
and deep space is the very depiction
in detail of God's face.
Knowledge born-is one birth
to save self
societies-ever-Living Fruit
need this breath.
With every digit and appendage
we extend it to provide proof
virtruvian man knowledge degree Supreme Alpha
A truth-in squares we the corner-
Stone skull and bone add on
to shine shrine home in my Sun Temp-le
and propel the excel of energy

we are the center of the sol-AR's
center those who fold dimensions into wormholes
and then enter
the balance of the flame and fluid
that levels the limbic to lucid
in ether where we hurl
photons to nourish neuros in grey matter
to your cingulate gyrus
and riding listeners amygdala
of virus such as fixed fiction
we are the Sun's center.

We Hail From The Center Of The Sun

Conversation piece: probe,
on higher frequencies with energy
to "G" force from your soul.
Seek the source when it's untold.
We unfold soles - gargantuan footprints
in space time continuum.
Maximum minimum millenniums
millions of maximilians
ga-zillions of celestial carthagians
genetic descendants descended from scrolls.
Helixing DNA codes
scattered through protoplasmatic skulls.
We've surgically removed Suns from solar systems
living victims
who's cosmic tissue spore galactic graveyards,
chariots of God's, like pyramids and myriads
of portals.
A womb like tomb to support the mortals
let them suckle on the breast of the immortals,
then call it advanced technology
technically it's average
when we average the advantage
in any technotronic age, era or movement
it's moodless like a moon's expression
yet we hail from the center of the Sun
we seek truth from the circumference
of the subconscious on all levels locked inside
of one.
Knowledge locks all sides of the Son
and the key keeps coming up
with depths deeper than the soul's sum.

We Hail From The Center Of The Sun

The highly fused elements called one!
ciphering nature eternally
from positions that parallel into diverse dimensions of cerebral artistry.
The dynamic break down unfolding in myriad spectrums that beam pass
the infinity of memory.
Every 25,000 years circling black holes that birth our celestial chemistry.
turning cosmic respiration into the medium that allows
mirroring mimicry.
Microcosmic energy holding its own.

"WE HAIL FROM THE CENTER OF THE SUN"

The "A"-zone!
Alphabetically numbered in digital tones,
that helix the glow neon and phone home
the wisdom of our over standing full blown
and grown by 23 chromosomes feeding off mind alone.
Powering pure refinement which to grafted clones seem unknow-

"WE HAILED FROM THE CENTER OF THE SUN"

And burn for you lessons of light that legion
beyond the magnitude of mortal consciousness
and make time yarn in a waiting weariness that yearns
for our return.
The Aliens of light obscured in darkness,
due to the lack of ability to spark it:
(your own perception!)
your own hell and obsession!
the pit that makes every man, woman and child weary:
(the pituitary!)
the G-land in your language called gland.
Where we the God's land to leave multiple universes connected by
synapse
of water, fire and sand.
That demand cultivation in 3's for the continuance of man.

"WE HAIL FROM THE CENTER OF THE SUN"

Leaving photonic footprints that indent curvatures in space time,
Incasing portions of mind that individually matrix Supreme design,
called relativity
and the laws that lead back to immaterial symmetry.
The intelligent intelligence manifesting light years in sequence,
to position and distance particles that article to articulate peace.
The etheric quarks chanting our increase by election release.

"WE HAIL FROM THE CENTER OF THE SUN"

And master intellectual agility by the fusion of self.
The "We" and "Us" becomes Nu and clear
as one appears and remain stealth
within vibrations that portal haphazardly into galactic belts.
writing the criterion of magnetism that causes you to praise us.
With centered thoughts and ultra violet rays
that appeal for the long awaited appearance of our faces.
The Lord, Abbot and Son.
The origin of all and one!

"WE HAIL FROM THE CENTER OF THE SUN"

Chapter four

Dedications

Supernova

In loving memory of: Lisa "Left Eye" Lopes

My left eye haunted
my premonitions
of an Honduran revolt.
My status as a human being
revoked.
So I vote, with hands on my throat.
The violence of domestic unhoped
squeezes a soul and continuously choke.
A lost love can't cope.
Provoked to scribble passionate notes
on my flesh, I confess
yes-my heart is broke.
My life ten shades of despair.
Pray God even care
cuz then all ten fades
into thin air.
If not...
Burn me along with my beliefs.
I'm so hot-
set this cruel world on fire
with the flames of grief,
the stains of mischief.
My pain intense and deep.
It' s a strain not to weep.
If I die don't wash my feet.
I'd rather be washed in peace.
Watch over my peeps
and watch and see,
pray I journey towards ecstasy.
And alcohol...it drowns the hurt.
Cursed to a wretched Earth.
On my knees clutching the dirt.
Please Lord! show me my worth.
Too <u>Tender</u> to be <u>Loved</u> without <u>Care.</u>

Home alone.
but I pretend
a soul to hug me is there.
Maybe if I was cool enough
to be <u>Crazy</u> and <u>Sexy</u>
I could find marriage
and not just someone to sex me.
Many things perplex me.
Why do we <u>Creep</u>
when our lovers love so heavily?
My <u>Red light Special</u>
ain't a <u>Waterfall.</u>
Love is being there
when her water falls.
A baby's scream fills the air
the sounds of your daughter's call.
If I crash and fall
don't cry at all.
Bury me under a <u>Waterfall</u>
to the sounds of T.L.C's <u>Waterfall.</u>
Cuz in the end,
the rainbow means-
God loves us all.

HEY TEE!

She synchronized winks and blew unsolicited kisses at me
her stature read anything but liberty.
I suspect that her screams for help wasn't at liberty to yell
so like hell she sent up smoke signals that spelled, yele!
Tear drops in my eyes
but not even an Ocean's cry could extinguish the fire in her bosom
nor could I.
Her inferno was internal, as was her past history
ever since murderous mercenaries murked her children.
No wonder she mourns
she's torn.
Damn them son's of bitches; uncircumcised individuals
who pealed back the resilience of her land like foreskin, I could just
kill them....
I wish I'd never seen her
her dross
her patina.
She wore a fleece that was flea riddled with infestation
her blood trickled from her nails from the scratching and itching.
She was sick of it; irate even
so she shook violently the bone structure of her body
until her entire island began to quake.
Woe is me!
I can see beneath her earth and what pain gave birth to.
The pestilence and poverty.
Empty pantries in mut hut shanties.
Eruptions of violence in volume that volcano's couldn't lava.
Polluted agendas.
Genocide and 90 lb women 9 months pregnant with twins.
Men with no hustle at all
but manage to muster up enough muscle to utter that musket ball.
Young Queens woofly flirting with many men
in hopes that they would come into her
but mentally those that prowled wasn't interested in her innocence
so instead they scrawled the inlay of her virgin island like perverted
tyrants

until they physically ripped her inlands apart.
I screamed....Rude Boy have a heart!
but there was no pardon allotted
just a continuous act of bloodshed and blood baths
from bloodshot eyed blood clots.
Bloodthirsty bloodsuckers that bloodhound their own blood-line
leaving behind blood trails from bloodcurdling severing of blood vessels-
what a bloody mess!
Bloodstains from the bloodstreams of young bloods
who open blood accounts with blood money to blood banks for fun.
Daughter's/son's!
don't believe that her afflictions were self inflicted
her people wasn't the cause of her diseases
her destruction had no visible reason
she was just sick and tired of breathing in the debris
the sea's and its merchants had driven in-
So she sneezed
So we could finally say, bless you Haiti.

The Poison of Art

He walked like Shaft to a harmonious hum,
instrumental drums native to blues and jazz.
Electric guitars and raspberry lights in acid parties.
Wore headbands like Jimmy Hendrix, helixing in half notes.
Banged out the American woman on American flags,
said he was sexing Marilyn Monroe between the sheets of
Rolling Stone mags.
It's hard to believe him
when he's sleeping in my mother's basement- face it-
the 70's got him wasted.
He looked at me and said
nobody loves like the 70's does, blood,
it sounded prophetic or poetic the way his words were.
His words slurred
birds emerged in a blur from his smoke.
I only heard a third of his joke
cause he laughed a thunderous choke,
and his last few words were something about him being broke
could he be metaphorically describing his soul
and what it's worth.
Or the energy it took for him
to go witness his second daughter's birth.
Crack cocaine was his first, but that's another story,
reliving his glory days in a daze, going out in a blaze
like Eddie Kane.
I'm glad he came like steady rain,
my man say he's an old player,
I just say players old.
I hate to see him this way
but player played from his soul.
He lost it in a Coupe
with a group of ex-prostitutes
that shoot heroin through their necks when it's cold.
This is my brother we're talking about,
but his story was destined to be told,
sold to a higher bidder

bidded with lost souls.
Strolled through grey areas of life
where unspeakable things bore holes.
The bars bent his spirit abit
now he lit his cigarettes with shaky hands,
blowing smoke as he talked,
said he walked the last 30yrs as a dead man.
the sound of keys became a close friend,
Said he couldn't get the jingling out his head.
So he sat next to the amp differentiating strings,
the cords don't sound the same anymore,
his music's a useless whore, pimped out in portions,
his songs out of proportion, melodic abortions,
he sang the lyrics to a song that poisoned art.

Lifts My Heart
A poem to my mother, Sharon

How can I express
the gratitude I feel.
I must confess
I think you're made of steel.
For you were strong
when I stumbled.
Pride steered me wrong.
Circumstances made me humble.
You amaze me daily
with your ability. Your energy
lifts my heart
when I drift towards the dark.
Mother, you are my spark
that encourages me
to finish whatever I start.

LOVES GOT A NAME

I celebrate the detection confirming the speculation acquainted with an
emotional
whirlwind.

The continued disagreement that reverberates through the ascending
comprehension of
the perplexed.

What I feel lacks a relatable identity & my experiences baffle the
understanding defined by the many teachers who assigned the lesson
plan.

I misunderstood & took the resemblance for the actual thing & in the
presence of
deficiency, I embraced scarceness out of sheer need.

But what I needed was defeated by the absolute once I received it and
now that I've
retrieved it, I'm free of those uncertain emotional chains, cause, Loves
got a name!

Loves got a name that's engraved permanently in my skin.
Inscribed for life directly into the definition of my "Softside".

I'm no longer misguided by the dysfunction of assumption.

I'm wrapped securely in the authenticity that overshadows the
misinterpretation
misinterpreted by the misinterpreted who interpreted it to me.

My accuracy is actually spelled with seven letters, not four.

My enunciation is "Brizhai," yours is" Love," but the affection is one in
the same.
Yours is just a word, mine has a name.

I once thought I was deprived of the affectionate affiliation connected
with the spiritual
connection manifested through the outpouring of devotion. But what I
found at truths
location was a treasure chest of dedications devoted to me & the
emulation carbon copied
for the world to see.

Unmatched by anything I've ever seen, I've often had to pinch myself to
assure myself that I wasn't living inside of a dream but now that my
imagination & reality reveals the same,

My 14 year conclusion is
Loves got a name!

A Mother's Love

Often yelled at and mistreated
prison life is what I'm seeing.
Bars slam and doors close
Only if you knew the secrets they hold.
Stuck in a world filled with madness
sad to say, besides my family there isn't much gladness.
Loud noises and screams fill the night
only to know there isn't a guard in sight.
No one care about the people that's here.
But a Mother's love is always near!

Dedication:

Mom I wrote this poem with you on my heart constantly
and appreciating your love now and forever.

WALK THIS WAY

Modesty hadn't yet magnified itself in Micahs destiny when she was 11, so, she spoke with destiny's focus when she told me,

"Daddy I'mma be a model someday"

Before I could corral her thoughts, she took off down this makeshift runway, throwing her undeveloped genetics the wrong way while humming that classic Aerosmith anthem.

"Walk This Way"

I damn near balked, but caught my reply before I let its meaning fly out of my mouth, see, I already had these preconceived thoughts about what a model meant to me, so I wasn't about to entertain thoughts about her entertaining without...clothes, you know; sparingly wearing feathery stoles on her naked shoulders, fish-net pantyhose and open toe stilettos,
All I envisioned was my Princess secrets peeking through Victoria Secrets when her secrets shouldn't have a peephole to peep through.
I see disturbing images of my Queen nursing stomach pangs, her frame weighing less than a fiend and she's bulimic because she made her two middle fingers her best friends.
I thought, "What type of father would I be if I allowed my seed to model, if I gave way for her to rip the runway and take strides so damaging to her character, that there's no way her way fare would survive,"

Would I be a road manager, or a role model?

I composed this thought while holding my composure, and for the first time, I turned to look in her eyes,
Then the answer came, "damn it! I am a father!"
Finally, I saw in her eyes what a model meant to her, and then I modified my way of thinking, hoping that I could sink into the essence of her chimera,
and like a camera, my minds lenses lent me access to access the way she walked, turned and snapped her neck, and like snap shots,

My mind snapped out a million reels of photogenic film, then took and developed their negatives into positives,

Now I'm positive that she will be a model,

so I reloaded my film, (digital), then refocused my mental lens and pulled the trigger,

"you will be a model someday"

But not like Tyra, you'll be a bit more towering, a monument like, Michelle Obama, see, when you strut your stuff, your stuff will have enough sustenance to sustain you, no need for extra stuffing, nip tucks, bo-tox and such,

Your pose alone will oppose the peekers, and your poise will put you in position to proposition and possess a king like Heidi Klum did,

and when your maids of honor throw rice on your wedding day, they will call you Condoleezza, while releasing doves in your honor, secretly debriefing your essence,

your smile is effervescent, combusting its luster into florescent blooms, igniting the boom! of your flash cube, NOW THAT'S FASHION!

The way you flash your God given talents, not by balancing books on your head and proper etiquette, but by putting books in your head,

See, the evidence of your relevance is in your walk, it is in what you say, not how you talk.

...so, sashay the way you see fit, and if you have to sass in any event, then sass with sense, but just don't run down runways without knowing your way, instead, dare to strike a pose for this heart and soul that truly care, and,

"walk this way"

Dedicated to my beautiful daughter: Micah A. Rush

Forbidden
To: Tina Michelle

It's hard
for a man
to talk about his heart
and not be, torn apart.
I've been torn from the start.
Sincerely search for a place to park.
A touch of grace
in this world of dark.
A warm face that sparks
a warm state
similar to Heaven and the stars.
I feel ensouled
like a South Korean in Seoul.
There's a feeling in my soul
that keeps me protected
like an insole.
When I was 15-years old
A soul-survivor
my pain went unconsoled,
my mortal heart froze and cold.
So I sold my soul.
Earned it back
only to have it stole
by the woman of my dreams.
A woman who means
a woman's worth.
The worth of a woman
determined by her work
with spiritual things.
You're my lyrical Queen.
My catalyst in Biblical things.
My heart in tangible shape.
What love creates
let no one break.

We can't deny fate.
Confident I can make
you shake like an earthquake.
Count your pleasures
by the eights, sixteen's, and thirty-two's.
Eliminate your emotional aches
and annihilate your mental blues.
Together we digest
what you psychologically ate.
Role play Adam and Eve,
the first mates.
Shower you with attention from the moment you wake.
You wouldn't even be
tempted to taste
the forbidden fruit preffered by that wicked snake.

THE WOUNDED HEART A.K.A. WENDY OSBOURNE

Time claims she heals all wounds,
Promises to numb the pain,
A perfect bandage ebbs the blood,
That flows from the severed vein,
But Time withheld her only prescription,
I'm remiss to ponder my painful plight,
Days and nights passing, no longer a solution,
For wounds that refuse to heal, no scar in sight,
Round and round hands spin indefinitely,
Though handicapped at changing fate,
Imagination dangles the unreal before me,
Taunting me to draw near,
And in this obscure realm I dwell,
Gazing at unfulfilled visions,
Aces and scenes played out differently,
Chances to bask in what could have been,
But pain snatches me from my dreams,
My smile begins to wane,
My wounds have walls, high and huge,
Holding me captive to my pain,
Why did I rely on Time? What did I hope she could do.
How did I think healing would come?
When passing Time is all that Time can do.

Jewel

In the beginning, there were Afrikaan Queens who sat opposite their Kings adorned with shiny things, bling that the earth yielded to them, but it wasn't the carats in their tiara's that facaded the worth in their facet's, it wasn't the glistening of rubies and sapphires that set fire to their beauty....they were born beautiful.

Joint rulers who stood by their Kings and in the shadow of his stature, her status cast shadows upon Princesses vying for her status. But somewhere along her lineage many women lost their footing and fell off that ladder, now in these latter-days our Princesses are afraid to rescale that ladder, so as a father, I battle my daughter fears and give Ashley the tools to rebuild. I instill the mental apparatus inclined to reconstruct the lattice that left spaces and gapes throughout many generations.

I fight with the strength of my kinsmen, that :I might, avenge her innocence. See, Reese, lent me the spear he inherited from his peers, so I can pierce the shields of them who chuck stones at my clone flesh and bones, and I'll blow darts at their heart before I let men cash in on her sweet-tarts---she be my sweetheart, the sweetsop that her mother squeezed out while screaming, "take it out!"

That's when my Queendom had come! the heir to my throne, but I wasn't there to place the coronet in accordance to the ordinance of tradition, instead, my splendor was held in submission under the authority of this prison----physically----not mentally, and trust me Ashley when I say,

"IT WASN'T YOUR FAULT"

It was my will to fight the fears that fought me with warriors skills that shackled me,

"IT WASN'T YOUR FIGHT"

And though my plight continues and my wrongs don't equal right, as a father I will with all my might face my responsibilities,

And you my Queen, will climb that ladder that has sat idle and bring back the virtue and value that your ancestresses possessed, because you are the jewel in their crest.

Dedicated to my beautiful daughter: Ashley S. Shellman

I Prayed For You
Dedicated to my Grandfather,
John P. Bellamy Sr., and his posterity.

Granddaddy
I'm writing
This to you
Because,
I had a conversation
With
Althea,
A few thoughts
I wanted
To express
To you.
Granddaddy
I haven't prayed
In a while,
But last night
I prayed for you.
I prayed
God restored your strength.
We suffer
When we focus
On the wrong thing.
Granddaddy
I haven't prayed
In a while
But last night
I prayed for you.
I prayed
Somehow, your faith
In the beauty
Of life
Become replenished
And prolific.
Granddaddy
I haven't prayed
In a while

But last Night
I prayed for you.
I want you to know
I desire that you do know
Love is...
Viola being there
When it counts.
A relationship
of decades.
A model
To your posterity.
I want you to know
Love is...
Yvonne, Samuel, and John Jr.
I want you to know
Love is...
Lucius, Allen, and Althea.
I want you to know
Love is...
Leola, Sharon, and Delores.
I want you to know
Love is...
Anthony, Shannon, and Corey.
Granddaddy
I want you to know
Love is...
your posterity
Being there when
It counts.
We shall
Remember and honor you.
With our every breath.
For without you
There would be
No us.
Granddaddy
We love you
Always.

SOFTSIDE

Evolution takes its name from the father of progress & the mother of
refashion and since
conversion collaborated with development, the formula for my elixir
came through the
mixture of XX & chromosome.

Ingestion through the outward projection of affection caused my
aggression to leak
purposefully from the laceration produced with the intent to annihilate
ignorance &
rejuvenate persistence.

Persistence formed a bond with resilience threading perseverance to
adherence & now
my brilliance calls me DADDY.

Old fads water & fertilize the rotting corpus of indoctrinated thought
aborted by the
important.

Distortion witnessed through the contortion of bifocal lenses, Garble
tunneled my vision
until the Princess gave me permission to redirect my position.

Now equipped with the mission to eliminate the distance that divides us!

I cling tight to the inner me, the "Ni'she" that replaced the shield &
assumed
responsibility of protecting me.

Not physically, but mentally she's my personal security. Securing
personally the
conscience in me that clears the paths that leads to her.

Hitch hiking antagonism could always find a ride, now they travel solo in
a leased minivan financed by my "SOFTSIDE".

The appointment made for the demolition of callousness made way for
the construction
of tolerant towers towering over temporary aggravation.

Tolerance breeds happiness & happiness manifest smiles, which means
my peace resides
in my pride.

My pride being "Brizhai" also known as my...

Softside

A Gentle Kiss

Dedicated to Adrianne and Crystal

Upon your pretty cheek
I place a gentle kiss.
Not only because I love you,
but because you are my sis.
Laughter fills me with happiness.
Love guides me towards joy.
Your smile has been written on
my heart with permanent ink.
I often toy with
the idea of life
without love. It leaves me remiss.
Makes me want to
give you a gentle kiss.

How Many Shotz?
Dedicated to: Sean Bell

Wounded by hot shotz
scatterin through
the dark streetz
one soul remainz unharmed
in my eyes
I saw the devil revealed
in the form of copz
fingerz pulling triggerz
life had no chance
inhalez and exhalez
of each breath became critical
and prayer began to deliver
tearz became blood tearz
hearing screamz
from my unborn child
my spiritual armz
reaching for peace
my wife covered wtih frost
frozen as she fell to her kneez
watching the bad newz
I got shot (50) timez!
and I didn't even commit a crime
LORD!
how many shotz?
how many blood tearz must I shed?
LORD!
tell the world
when will this police holocaust stop
never got a red light
sparkz was all I saw in my eyez
those last dayz
evading those killerz
that were suppose to
serve and protect

instead
I'm left to cope paralyzed inside
and my corpse
is trapped filled with holez
since a seed
my death was written
did you forget that
I had dreamz and goalz in life?
stereotyped by a modern klan
gangbangerz, drug dealerz, ect-
echoing inside these devils headz
LORD!
how many shotz?
how many blood tearz must I shed?
tell the world
when will this police holocaust stop.
killerz acquitted
while my family memberz continue to
seek civil liberty
in a land that's so hypocritical
gun powder polluting the air
lifting my soul from my body
don't worry mama
I felt no pain
my spitirual handz
will wipe away your physical tearz
and heal your wounded heart
childhood memories will give you
strength and motivation to put
to cease these new wayz of lynching
LORD!
HOW MANY SHOTZ?
how many blood tearz must I shed?
LORD! Tell the world
When will this police holocaust stop?

P.E.A.C.E.

I first give sincere acknowledgement to the Most High; who resides in all the minds and hearts of the true and living.

My honorable name is Julius Ivy, but most refer to me by my divine title of: "Intelligent. Sun. Universal. Allah. (I. Sun for short.)"

I was dropped into the plane of flesh 6-4-82. My magnetic destiny towards greatness has brought me to this degree in time to reveal the conditions of mind, from which all life derives. My composure of experiences and visualizations occur from my environments and the many found and lost souls who I've encountered. Life has positioned me to grow from the vile demographics of Chicago's west side. Where the poor choices only allow two outcomes; that being jail or death.

Unfortunately my poor decisions has given me 15 years of incarceration. Yet mercy is an event dynamically expressed by my change. The oppressive environments, (ghetto & prison) has stimulated a revolution of Self, Mind and Spirit.

My dissatisfaction spawns a pure inspiration for any free expression of mind. Simply because it's the creative forces we call art, but on a deeper level, is seem to be the divine working through us.

The very nature of art whether written or spoken, drawn or done through dance, reveals the power of truth, which is one harmonizing self with the universe to bestow its beauty. For this cause I emerge to give what's held.

I would like to give a special thanks to Kuta and Reese, who was the brain Childs behind what you now hold. And to all the writers who took the time to bestow their gift of thought. Peace to all the Gods and Earths!

> The young Enlightener!
> P.E.A.C.E.
> UP COMING PROJECTS:
> Inspirational book: "Striving 2 leave a legacy."

Celestial Helix

The pollution of my rhythm placed a genetic blues
within my bones,
which made my song undecipherable.
Like turbulent souls yearning to comprehend a
light unable to explore.
Misdirected hate steadies my heart rate,
on a scale were disease: causes cancer,
high blood pressure and stress to quote my fate.
Hyperventilating with my pen for an expression
that provides harmony within.
BUT HATE!...."Hate" sways in the
stream of every vein.
Condensing my every nerve and cell with pain
until it flows without.
Into a society of doubt,
where unwanted sobriety allows me to enter its mouth,
to be inhaled by its nose and tasted with its tongue
embraced by its lungs until its cerebral is rung
by the rhythm of my drums.
A **snare** of ungodliness.
A **bam**! of sexism.
A **tap** of blindness to repel the exorcism.
And a bop of hate for my own to pollute the
rhythm in their bones.
Can you feel it!?
Vibrating the youths from wombs gyrating to lust's
penetrating **boom**!!?
Well if you can't feel it then maybe you
can help heal it!
All you have to do is replay the song in your
Celestial Helix!

BIO

My name is, Selma Butler, and I'm from Chicago IL. I'm a 32 year old writer who really enjoy what I do. So when I was asked to be a part of "OutCreye"---the line-up, I gratefully accepted.

Opportunity such as this don't come very often. I'm currently in the process of co-writing a book titled, (Project Parables) with Mario Moss. Hopefully It'll be in the stores mid 2011 so that the world can enjoy what we have to offer.

To the founder and Co-founders of S.W.P. Maurice Reese Hayes and Robert Kuta Rush as well as K.T. thank you for helping me understand that goals give meaning to life.

Grateful am I to the man that stir my thoughts.

WHAT NEXT?

When the Sun met the corner Father Lord forgive them
Pacman in the field with a sack picking that cotton
Lifestyle of the old negro gone but not forgotten
Shackled to street dreams, teens find and chase an American folklore
Young bucks chasing dollars, and running from change
Ain't no pay back of souls, from black lives sold
Our past struggles are our today's troubles
We're slaves of economics, prisoners of politics, and poorly educated
Shots are being fired at a black nation
Screams of our Mothers, echo a child-less to the American dream
Understand, we're living life with no real means,
We're pawns in no good positions
The plantation was a training phase, corn rows of negros, still a good
crop
House niggas in the police station, and the field negro in the streets
They say, strong black men is a dying breed
So should I label myself a endangered species, who welfare depends on
government assistance
Our world• is strange, we adapted ourselves to their hate and crime
black on black---penitentiary packed
We're infecting ourselves like Tuskegee wasn't enough
we experiment with drugs, and then try them out on our communities
Claimed the streets then divided ourselves like blocks
Civilians with Civil Rights committing Civil War
It started with clubs and knives, fist fights and bites
Then the heavy artillery came
along with the gangsta nicknames.

What next?

BIO

My name is Mario Moss, I'm a Chicago native. I'm 35 years old, my passion is writing and it's also therapy, something I must do to keep a peace of mind.

My style of writing comes from within. I literally can write only when my mind need to let something go.

So I share with you my experiences and how I perceive life. It's a personal goal I've always had to share my thoughts with the world to leave something behind after I'm gone.

It wasn't my intention to team up and write with someone else, but life presented me with an opportunity that I think fits into what I want to accomplish. I teamed up with a person that makes me do what I do better, so we came up with the idea for "Project Parables".

It's a team effort whereas we critique each other's work to make sure our best effort is being put out. We plan to have our first book out in 2011, so we hope that you'll enjoy this introduction to what's to come.

Our styles as you can see is very versatile, I think everyone can enjoy what we have to bring to the table.

Some pieces are written solely by me, others by him and some we finished where the other left off, which I love sometimes because my mind might go blank, and he can clear it with no problem.

In closing, I hope that everyone enjoy this book and look for future works from each writer. I also want to thank Kuta and Reese for allowing "Project Parables" to appear in their righteous endeavor, that's a good look.

What will they say!

When your dollars reach a drizzle
and all the raining cease
when the Sun shed light and the Earth swallow tears of the mourning
what would they say of you?
ask yourself was your life worth the nine months of hurt and strain
or facial expressions of your Momma's pain
did beauty have to bother or bare a burden just to conceive a beast
ask yourself?
think about the heartache she felt when she held you in her arms
she didn't have your daddy so she just gave you his name
brought you up with love because she didn't have a cent or sense
to give you away, so she and her mother raised you
now what games do you want to play....
ask yourself before life seeks its refund
and calls to count the favors you've mishandled
what will they say after your gone?
when your son grow up and learn from his Mom about world views
and all she ever told him was Dad was bad news
what will they say when the community in all its poverty and crime
ask what you contribute besides dealing drugs to your neighbors
or violence to their daughters
What will they say when you're on trial and the jury is not of your peers
hears statements from character witnesses
what responsibility will you take
when you never stood on anything as a man
you was the boy that the white man named you
you took after the bastard that never claimed you
is that what they'll say after you're gone?

BIO

My name is Omar Halim Suphice. I was born and raised on the South Side of Chicago. Writing poetry has always been a way for me to relax and free my mind. Therefore, as long as I'm alive, I will never stop sharing my creative designs with the world.

I want to thank Maurice Hayes "Reese" and Robert Rush "Kuta" for allowing my poetic thoughts to appear in print and thank Allah, the Most Gracious and Most Merciful for allowing me to exist.

HUGGING A STAR

A park bench somewhere in the autumn we rest
content with each other, snuggled up tight.
Imagine us on a crispy clear night.
You in my arms with your head on my chest.
To cuddle with you will make me feel blessed-
like there is nothing in the world more right
than us two together enjoying life
 on a park bench somewhere plotting our nest
and wondering about the things beyond.
Like can two possibly love from afar,
develop something so strong like a bond.
(Shared between where we imagine we are.)

On a park bench somewhere where we are fond
of watching the sky, I'm hugging a star.

Sonnet

Bio

My journey begun in 1980, I'm the middle child of three babies. Children Memorial Hospital, Chicago Illinois is where my parents birthed me. As a young lad I was as hard headed as a NFL helmet; Bay-Bay kid was something I heard very often. Ironically Bay-Bay is my mother's nick name; one in the same not having my big brother around gave me a reason to act like a clown.

My father was born in Mississippi and at the age of fifteen he entertained a dream of moving to Chicago. Well his dream came true, but little did he know he would be forced to live as an adult. My father was like my best friend, the word discipline was not in his vernacular. In essence he provided the bullet proof vest. There was nothing I could not get away with, he protected me.

My life made a turn for the worst, so I thought for twelve years I have been adapting to life on the inside. While on the inside the deaths of my parents changed my prospective on life. Losing my parents to drugs compelled me to look within myself , in my quest I discovered I was selfish and impatient. Patience arrived with me sharing myself with my siblings Rook & Skeet. My love for them created a bond only my mother's imagination could meet.

I witnessed a lot of passion & creative writing by men with a pen while in the penitentiary I was inspired by their poetry thus throwing my ideas around in my mind. I decided to feed my alter ego to express what I have been suppressing for years---bottled emotions and fears.

My emotions flowed like water in a river thus causing my pen to bleed, composed from the heart, I released tears of fear. I write to release bottled pain, maybe its divine and because my name is Arthur it's a form of Art I now could claim as my own.

My Momma never told me...And My Poppa never showed me!!!

My Momma never told me about Ms Promiscuous and her list of many men. Love once was a friend or better yet a next to Kin.

Passionately, I performed my art between her bed sheets. When we would role play she'd call me Mr. Longpete, was it because of my longevity or the Sir name of her longest partner?

Goodbyes in our departure never took place, I compared myself to a pair of her Red bottom heels. I got used, walked around, thrown to the side. Thank God Ms. Promiscuous didn't leave me with a STD in our final bye-bye.

While pondering the consistence of my pride, I realized Poppa never showed me how to stride with swagger in the presence of a bona fide woman.

Poppa would perejaculate mentally amid procuring his ladies, treating them with disrespect. His misogynistic demeanor strips them of their worth. What's worse is that they believed they only belonged in the kitchen or on a corner in a skirt.

Beneath his skin within the cavity of his chest was a heart pumping blood at 40 degree below zero. He had no knowledge of his mother's hero, so how could he show me how to go with no growth in his profile.

My Momma never told me how our family came from glory, our history lives through my great grand Father's story. He was the epitome of an entrepreneur before becoming an entity. He survived treacherous times in 1929.

Success is a word my Momma never told me of, Webster was the Poppa who showed me how to define it. However if I had to split Moms and Pops wits, my Momma was a witty writer who told me to aim higher. And witty Poppa showed me how to stay paid in many ways.

My success today is defined by how successful I am at sharing myself with the world despite its multiple colors.

My Momma never told me... And my Poppa never showed me, but I am who I am suppose to be.

Bio

King Shamik Divine Justice Allah was born and raised in C-medina (Chicago) while living in an area call the Kingdom of Truth (K-Town).

Being a part of the Nation of Gods & Earth plus being a long time follower, listener, and student of Hip Hop inspire many of my concepts. Although social issues, family, my better half, and a constant search of bringing consciousness to our people are my motivation to place those concepts on paper. Peace to the Gods, Earths, and all of the positive people of the universe.

MY WORD

Picture my word and think on just how it got you to listen to me.
Through my word we can build a better future by knowing the history.
My word is rawer than the five elements and can never be tamed.
In fact my word should be known as the sixed one that can't be explained.

Within my word knowledge is to build being born all is equal to power.
From truth all lies my word was specifically created to devour.
There is no alpha or omega my word existed before the beginning and has no ending.
Even without a start or end my word lives in everything dead or living.

My word is spoken of well and always mentioned in every major religion.
This word is to being strength in death, life, and even through prison.
Power to the people and my word was the birth of something to believe in.
Throughout eternity even my unspoken word has been known as the voice of reason.

My word is bond and my bond is my life I'd rather give my life before my bond is broken.

In hearing or reading this you're envisioning the masses waiting for my word to be spoken.

My word is forever the essence and the essence is forever my word.
The loving word was to breathe life into everything you've know or heard.
The all mighty within the most known and powerful signs broke my word is divine.
Verbalization brings about a sensation so simple but complex is my word design.
My word is holy meaning un-tampered with and needs no purification.
The word is potent so be wise not to over dose on it like medication.

Be very careful because my word is livin' to any that choose to hear it.
My word will not be sugar coated, watered down, or diluted in the mix.

My word has before been sadly mistaken of being foreign even alien.
Until mathematics and science showed that my word was drafted from within.

My word has been spoken and was more than able to give the blind sight.
Through the darkness my word was able to lead the deaf, dumb, and blind to the light.
My word is the most honorable universal key to unlock mental and physical chains.
Through my word the dumb are freed and taught to use their brains.

My word existed before me and will exist long after I'm gone.
Like walking on three legs, my word is that staff that truth stands on.
My word has been used to strike fear into the most powerful nations.
These words can be used to either build or destroy causing major devastation.

So many times it has felt like my word is all that I ever had left.
It was my word that has brought comfort to the world as it wept.
It is the knowledge in my word that motivates life even within a last breath.
My word is the tool that allows the babies to develop and take first steps.

Now I ask can you understand the words that flow from my mental.
In the long run the word you've just witnessed will become an issue.
Word to the wise, if you do not take heed to the wise word,
You just may utter that my word told me so as your last words.

You may order more copies of this book and/or copies of Robert's first book, Outcreye The Rebirth as well as other books brought to you by Spit With A Purpose by using this order form or logging onto:

MidnightExpressBooks.com

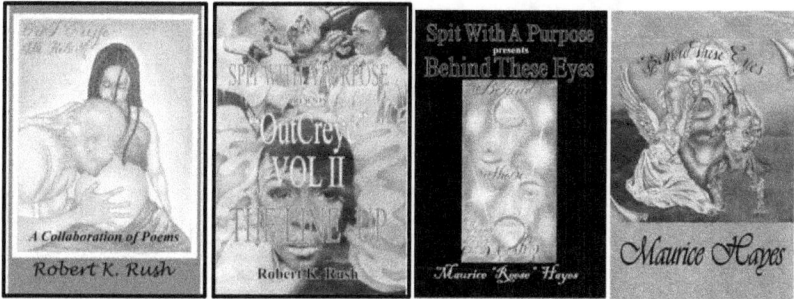

QTY	Title	Price Each	
_____	OUTCREYE – The Rebirth	$10.00	_____
_____	OUTCREYE Vol II - The Line-Up	$14.95	_____
_____	BEHIND THESE EYES	$ 8.00	_____
_____	BEHIND THESE EYES Vol II	$12.00	_____

Shipping
___ books ordered @ $3.99/Each   _____

TOTAL ENCLOSED   _____

Please send check or money order to:

Midnight Express Books
POBox 69
Berryville, AR 72616

NAME: _____

ADDRESS: _____

CITY: _____ STATE _____ ZIP _____